Psychoanalysis and the Future of Global Politics

Robert Samuels

Psychoanalysis and the Future of Global Politics

Overcoming Climate Change, Pandemics, War, and Poverty

Robert Samuels
Writing Program
University of California, Santa Barbara
Santa Barbara, CA, USA

ISBN 978-3-031-41165-6   ISBN 978-3-031-41166-3 (eBook)
https://doi.org/10.1007/978-3-031-41166-3

© The Editor(s) (if applicable) and The Author(s), under exclusive licence to Springer Nature Switzerland AG 2023

This work is subject to copyright. All rights are solely and exclusively licensed by the Publisher, whether the whole or part of the material is concerned, specifically the rights of translation, reprinting, reuse of illustrations, recitation, broadcasting, reproduction on microfilms or in any other physical way, and transmission or information storage and retrieval, electronic adaptation, computer software, or by similar or dissimilar methodology now known or hereafter developed.

The use of general descriptive names, registered names, trademarks, service marks, etc. in this publication does not imply, even in the absence of a specific statement, that such names are exempt from the relevant protective laws and regulations and therefore free for general use.

The publisher, the authors, and the editors are safe to assume that the advice and information in this book are believed to be true and accurate at the date of publication. Neither the publisher nor the authors or the editors give a warranty, expressed or implied, with respect to the material contained herein or for any errors or omissions that may have been made. The publisher remains neutral with regard to jurisdictional claims in published maps and institutional affiliations.

This Palgrave Macmillan imprint is published by the registered company Springer Nature Switzerland AG.
The registered company address is: Gewerbestrasse 11, 6330 Cham, Switzerland

Paper in this product is recyclable.

Dedicated to my daughter and the future

Contents

1. Introduction: Psychoanalysis and Future of Global Progress 1
2. *The Future of an Illusion* and the Conservative Rejection of Globalization 15
3. The Left's Critique of Psychoanalysis and Globalization 33
4. Psychoanalyzing the Right's Rejection of Globalization 51
5. Globalization and its Discontents: Revisiting the Critique of the Centrist Global Elites 73
6. Conclusion: Psychoanalysis and the Psychology of Global Enlightenment 93

Index 109

CHAPTER 1

Introduction: Psychoanalysis and Future of Global Progress

Abstract This book offers a unique approach by using Freudian psychoanalytic theory to explain how we can resolve the most important issues facing the world today and in the future. One of my main arguments is that we need to move beyond national politics in order to provide global solutions to global problems. However, there is a misplaced fear concerning global governance, and much of this phobia is derived from a misunderstanding of history and human psychology. Not only do we have to learn to give up our idealized investment in nations and nationalism, but we also have to move beyond seeing the world from the perspective of a victim fantasy. Since we often repress real signs of global progress, we experience the global present and the future in negative ways. To reverse this perspective, we should first understand the incredible progress humans have made in the last two hundred years, but we also should not ignore the real threats we face.

Keywords Nationalism • Global progress • Global politics • Freud • Psychoanalysis • Victim fantasy • Climate change • Universal human rights

This book offers a unique approach by using Freudian psychoanalytic theory to explain how we can resolve the most important issues facing the world today and in the future. One of my main arguments is that we need to move beyond national politics in order to provide global solutions to global problems. However, there is a misplaced fear concerning global governance, and much of this phobia is derived from a misunderstanding of history and human psychology. Not only do we have to learn to give up our idealized investment in nations and nationalism, but we also have to move beyond seeing the world from the perspective of a victim fantasy. Since we often repress real signs of global progress, we experience the global present and the future in negative ways. To reverse this perspective, we should first understand the incredible progress humans have made in the last two hundred years, but we also should not ignore the real threats we face.[1]

To clarify why we are not acting on climate change and other pressing problems, I discuss our misunderstandings and the psychoanalytic process of denial.[2] Linked to this defense mechanism is the Freudian concept of the death drive and the relation between repression and the unconscious. I also describe how our lack of understanding is supplemented by conspiracy theories derived from the primary processes.[3] Ultimately, we should embrace Freud's theories of the reality principle and neutrality in order to fully understand how to pursue global progress in the future through the extension of universal human rights and unbiased science.[4]

Book Outline

Drawing from Steven Pinker's *Enlightenment Now*, I begin with a brief description of the evidence and causes of global progress. After establishing what has and has not worked in the past to extend human lifespans, I examine current and future threats to our shared world. I also focus on what psychological processes block us from comprehending the past and the future on both an individual and a collective level. Through the Freudian concept of victim fantasy, I describe how we often repress the truth of our global progress.[5]

Chapter 2 provides a close reading of Freud's *The Future of an Illusion* in order to comprehend the premodern conservative ideology that still limits global progress today.[6] Freud's often neglected text provides a psychoanalytic understanding of the foundations of all social orders and the way that social hierarchies are established to protect the powerful and exploit the disempowered. As one of the leading sources for resistances to globalization, conservative ideology needs to be exposed and countered by the affirmation of scientific reason, universal human rights, and economic modernization. Moreover, we shall see that this move away from premodern institutions and beliefs is already being accomplished, but we need to understand how to peacefully continue the development of global Enlightenment.[7] At the heart of this chapter is how we need to change the way we think about nature and climate change.

In Chapter 3, I turn my focus to a Left-wing criticism of globalization and psychoanalysis. By examining Gary Walls "Toward A Critical Global Psychoanalysis," I discuss many of the reasons for the Leftist rejection of both global capitalism and psychoanalysis.[8] We shall see that one of the central aspects of the rejection of global progress and Freud's model of treatment is a misunderstanding of neutrality in psychoanalysis, science, and democratic law. Instead of seeing neutrality as a necessary but impossible ideal, the Left tends to dismiss this foundation of modernity because of its failure to be fully achieved.[9] By not only focusing on inequality, this chapter examines the role that globalization plays in countering poverty on an international level.

While Chap. 2 focuses on the conservative reaction to modern globalization, and Chap. 3 looks at the Left-wing critique of global progress, Chapter 4 examines the psychological and political roots of the Right-wing rejection of global solutions to global problems. Through a critical analysis of Glenn Beck's *The Great Reset*, I articulate the underlining borderline personality psychopathology underlying Right-wing conspiracy theories.[10] At its most fundamental level, the libertarian Right simply denies the need to act on climate change, pandemics, poverty, and the spread of dangerous weapons.

Although some of the critiques coming from the Left and the Right concerning globalization are based on actual facts, these reactions often suffer from misunderstanding both the negative and positive aspects of modern capitalism, democracy, science, and psychoanalysis. One reason for this distorted view of modernity is that centrist global elites have often presented a fake version of liberalism.[11] To help reveal the problematic psychopathology shaping these centrists, I interpret Joseph Stiglitz's *Globalization and Its Discontents* as a psychoanalytic mode of critical introspection.[12] In other words, Stiglitz exposes the internal conflicts of "centrist" global elites by attacking his own role in building a new global system.

The final chapter focuses on how we can help promote global solutions to global problems through a better understanding of psychoanalysis and universal subjectivity. Through a critique of Michael Shermer's *The Moral*

Arc, I discuss the danger on basing our understanding of global progress on evolutionary psychology and other pseud-sciences.[13] Instead of turning to the new brain sciences to discover what type of psychology best fits universal human rights and modern science, I argue that psychoanalysis represents the most effective science and philosophy for our global future. While I do not center each chapter on a particular global threat, I do show how the only way to address effectively climate change, pandemics, poverty, and war is to take on a universal form of subjectivity, which aligns with the role of neutrality in Freudian psychoanalysis.

Documenting Global Progress

The first step in understanding global progress is to address the clearest evidence of advancement. As Steven Pinker highlights in *Enlightenment Now*, perhaps the most indisputable fact is that over the last 150 years (1873–2023), the average global life expectancy has gone from 35 years to 70 years.[14] Before, we get to the causes for this increase in life expectancy, I want to first discuss many of the other top signs of global progress presented by Pinker.

Although many people believe that global poverty is increasing, the reality is that in the last two hundred years (1820–2020), the level of dire poverty as measured by the UN has moved from 90% of the world population to 10% (87).[15] Moreover, half of this improvement has occurred since 1980, and one of the greatest surprises is that as the global population has continued to increase, the level of extreme poverty has decreased.

During this time of international poverty reduction, we have also witnessed a major increase in the number of people living under democratic rule. Pinker documents how in 2015, a majority of world's population benefited from the rights and protections afforded by modern liberal democracies, and another third of the world's population was in countries governed by a mixture of democratic and autocratic states (203). If we look back in time, we find that in 1900, only a fifth of the world's population were in democracies, and in 1850, the number was seven percent. Even though we may be currently witnessing a backlash against modern liberal democracies, the global trend is heading towards international democratization. In fact, the vast majority of the people living outside of democracy reside in China (203).

As another symbol of global progress, Pinker highlights how we are currently seeing a major decrease in capital punishment, and as more and more countries outlaw the death penalty, the number of nations that execute people has been lowered to less than one fifth of the world's nations (209). During this same period, a real reduction in state-sanctioned racism and ethnic prejudice has been achieved. Pinker documents how in 1950, half of the countries in the world had laws discriminating against ethnic or racial minorities, but by 2003, that number had dropped to less than one fifth. Of course, there is still a long way to go on this front, but it is important to recognize the progress we have made as we strive for further improvement. If we do not document the real achievements, then we will not believe that we can improve things in the future.

One of the greatest improvements during the last two hundred years has been the increase in rights and opportunities for females. Few people realize that in 1900, only one nation allowed women to vote, and now, women can vote in every country except for the Vatican City (222). Pinker also points out that women now make up over 40% of the global workforce and a fifth of the members of national parliaments (222). Surprisingly, global polls have found that more than 85 percent of respondents claim that they support full equality for women.

In terms of global literacy, the rate has now moved from 10% in 1800 to 83% today. Most of the increase has occurred in the last fifty years, and a big factor is the education of females and people outside of Western Europe (236). For Pinker, literacy plays a role in a wide-range of social and personal areas:

> Studies of the effects of education confirm that educated people really are more enlightened. They are less racist, sexist, xenophobic, homophobic, and authoritarian. They place a higher value on imagination, independence, and free speech. They are more likely to vote, volunteer, express political views, and belong to civic associations such as unions, political parties, and religious and community organizations. They are also likelier to trust their fellow citizens—a prime ingredient of the precious elixir called social capital. (235)

Although it is hard to untangle correlation from causation, there is ample evidence that literacy and education are key drivers for global progress.[16]

As countries around the world dedicate more funding to education, they have also increased their spending on social welfare programs. Pinker reveals that a hundred years ago, developed nations on average dedicated 1% of their wealth to supporting children, the poor, and the aged, and this number has now shot up to 25% (322). It is important to realize that when more countries do more to help the disadvantaged, expectations grow around the world for an enhanced safety net, and the failures to achieve improved support become more evident.

A major reason why people are living longer is the spread of medicine, medical technology, and science-based medicine. Pinker emphasizes that smallpox, which killed over 300 million people in the twentieth century, no longer exists, and many other life-threatening diseases and infections are now being reduced and eradicated (64). Moreover, different practices, like sterilization of operating rooms, have served to save millions of lives all over the world. Although some see the massive deaths caused by the COVID-19 pandemic as a sign that our healthcare systems are failing, the fact of the matter is that things could have been much worse.[17]

The use of science to improve lives is also evident in the "green revolution" in agriculture: It is estimated that Carl Bosch's and Fritz Haber's development of fertilizer saved over 2.7 billion lives (75). Due to the development of new technologies through scientific experimentation, we are not only living longer, healthier lives, but we are also gaining time for leisure and other activities. In fact, due to new technologies, the amount of time people spend on housework has been reduced from 58 hours a week in 1900 to 15.5 hours in 2011 (251).

Perhaps the greatest indicator of global progress is the massive decrease of people dying from war, accidents, and other non-medical causes. Since 1980, the number of individuals losing their lives in wars has gone down 75%, and this number has been decreasingly steadily over time. We also have witnessed a major decrease in people dying from automobile accidents, plane crashes, fires, drownings, and workplace injuries (323). Most of these reductions in deathrates have been the result of government regulations and laws, and many of these governmental remedies have been caused by collective action and social movements.

The Causes for Success

Pinker argues that the three driving forces behind this story of global progress are reason, science, and humanism, and yet, I do not think he does a very good job at describing the meaning of these causes. To clarify his argument, I will first give a short intellectual history of global progress. This story begins with the three primary institutions of pre-modern life: religion, monarchy, and feudalism. While premodern religion is centered on the belief in the power of a single supernatural power to control the world, monarchy represents the belief in the power of a single human being to control a collection of people, and feudalism entails a predetermined social hierarchy.[18] These three systems of social organization reinforce each other, and they all point to a world centered on tradition, belief, and conservativism. They also almost always rely on a set of hierarchies that place men over women, adults over children, humans over animals, white people over people of color, and humans over nature.[19] What then happens with the birth of modern culture is that all of these premodern institutions and hierarchies are undermined by a commitment to the ideals of social equality, universal reason, and free individualism.

In the modern globalizing world, science replaces religion, democracy replaces monarchy, and capitalism replaces feudalism.[20] These replacements do not happen all at once or in a complete way all over the world, but these transformations do occur in one direction. In other words, once people experience the benefits of science, democracy, and capitalism, they rarely go back to the premodern alternatives.[21] Moreover, the world as a whole is becoming more scientific, democratic, and capitalistic, even if there are backlashes and resistances.[22]

The overall argument here is that people live longer, healthier lives when they rely less on religion and more on science to make important decisions about their lives.[23] To understand this claim, we have to first determine what we mean by modern science, which can be defined as the use of reason to examine the truth of reality in a neutral and unbiased manner.[24] It is important to stress that this form of modern science relies on the commitment to a set of necessary but impossible human ideals: One has to pursue truth and reality by trying at all times to be neutral and unbiased. Thus, unlike premodern belief systems based on tradition, faith, and fate, the modern thinker tries to eliminate all assumptions and prejudices in order to approach reality with an open mind. Moreover, this definition of science relates to the core of democratic law, which is also centered on the need to approach each case without bias.[25] Likewise, modern capitalism represents a system of economic exchange that is supposed to be universal and impersonal because the exchange value is not based on how people feel about particular groups of people.[26]

As many post-modern thinkers and critics argue, it is impossible to be purely objective, neutral, and unbiased, and yet, I would argue that the goal is to strive to attain these values by being aware of how we fail to live up to them.[27] In fact, the central cause of our global progress is our use of these ideals that have been created by humans and embodied in particular institutions and practices, like universities, courts, and laboratories.[28] Furthermore, the postmodern criticism pointing to real cases of bias and discrimination should be seen as necessary components to the pursuit of these modern ideals. In short, we need people to point out when we fail to live up to our ideals, so that we can continue to pursue our ideals in a more consistent and effective manner. For instance, post-modern social movements promoting gender equality are necessary to help us realize the modern ideals of democratic equality.[29]

Psychoanalysis and Globalization

The major reason why psychoanalysis plays a key role in promoting global progress is that Freud's theory and practice is grounded on the ideal of neutrality.[30] Just as we want our legal judges to be impartial and our scientists to be without bias, psychoanalytic treatment only works if the patient speaks without self-censoring, and this means that people have to learn to be impartial to their own thoughts and feelings. Furthermore, what enables this suspension of bias by the patient is the analyst's refusal to judge.[31] The neutrality of the patient and the analyst is thus the driving force behind psychoanalysis, and yet many analysts, therapists, and psychiatrists have given up on this ideal.[32]

For Freud, the practice of neutrality derives from what he calls the reality principle, which entails the ability of people to be radically honest with themselves as they give up their various defense mechanisms.[33] In fact, Freud compares reality testing to a process of mourning since we often have to confront not only the upsetting reality of loss, but we also have to stop investing emotionally in the lost object.[34] On a basic level, Freud posits that all individual change requires mourning and reality testing, which can be made possible through free association and critical introspection.

To help clarify this psychoanalytic understanding of change, I want to discuss my own transformation that was triggered by reading Pinker's book. Before I read his work, I had no idea about how much global progress has been made in so many different areas during the last two hundred years. Like many other academic critics on the Left, I thought that the world was getting worse in all areas, and because global capitalism had created so much inequality and poverty, there was no way for things to get better.[35] While reading his work, I found that many of my basic assumptions were challenged, and even though I did at first resist the facts he presented, I eventually changed my mind.

Since on a basic level, education is about changing minds, it is important to comprehend how this type of transformation is possible and what defense mechanisms often block it.[36] In other words, we not only need to change the world, but we also have to change ourselves. Since a major reason why we do not continue to pursue global progress is that we do not think it is possible, we need to think about how we disregard the reality of what has happened in the past. From a psychoanalytic perspective, it is vital to examine why we refuse to accept positive news about our shared past, and why do we prefer to see the world through the lens of negativity?

Hysterical History

One lesson we can draw from psychoanalysis is that people often fantasize about being victims.[37] Although there are really people who are victimized and oppressed in our world, it is important to analyze why someone would see themselves and the world around them from such a negative perspective. In his studies of hysteria, Freud found that people often imagine their suffering and illnesses, and often this sense of displeasure was derived from a fundamental fantasy.[38] At first, Freud thought that all of his female patients had been sexually assaulted by their fathers, but later, in a very controversial move, he affirmed that some of them only fantasized about being abused.[39] He then had to confront the question of why would someone imagine their own abuse?

Freud found that when one complained about suffering, one was able to remove oneself from social obligations and responsibilities.[40] He also discovered that suffering could become the sole focus of one's attention. In enlarging and extending his theory, I have posited that victim identity and identification is one of the most powerful forces in human history.[41] After all, most religions are founded on a fundamental scene of victimization (crucifixion, martyrdom, enslavement), and most wars begin by one country declaring its victim status. One reason why the turn to victim identity is so powerful is that it provides meaning and identity. Moreover, the revenge of the pure and innocent victim is justified, and it is wrong to criticize the victim.

In terms of our repression of global progress, we prefer on a personal and collective level to see the world through the fantasy-frame of victimization where there is a clear good "us" and an equally clear evil "them."

As Freud insisted, not only does suffering often create unity through empathy and identification, but the shared hatred of an evil other can be the foundation of a strong group bond.[42] As a form of splitting, the strict opposition between the victim and the perpetrator creates a reductive form of meaning, identity, and group identification.[43] In turn, this splitting helps people to avoid anxiety, ambivalence, and ambiguity as the world is seen in "black and white."[44] In fact, at the foundation of all conservative, premodern social orders, we find a set of binary oppositions shaping a social hierarchy, which provide order and stability for the culture.[45]

Since modern globalization is based on suspending tradition, faith, fate, and belief so that the world can be seen without bias or discrimination, it is easy to see why conservatives would reject a secular liberal democratic globalized world. However, it is still unclear why people on the Left would also reject evidence of global progress? A possible response for this question is that Left-wing thinkers and critics desire to reduce the suffering that remains in the world, and so in order to gain influence and support, they must focus on the victims of our world.[46] Furthermore, as we shall see, there is a real need for minority-based social movements to expand who is protected by universal human rights, and thus there is a dialectical relationship between modern democratic law and postmodern social movements. However, the need for the Left to focus on the negative often results in a rejection of the evidence of global progress and the modern institutions of science and democratic law.

Not only do conservatives and the Left tend to dismiss global progress and modern liberal democracy, but we are also witnessing a growing Right-wing attack on modern globalization.[47] As I will document, part of this rejection of global progress is based a fear of totalitarianism and a lost sense of individual identity.[48] There is also a strong influence of wealthy individuals and corporations that seek to avoid taxation and regulation. Yet, drawing from Freud's theory of the pleasure principle, I posit that underlying these different Right-wing responses, we find a denial of reality and a desire to hold onto Oedipal enjoyment.[49] From this perspective, the Oedipus Complex represents the way that individuals seek to pursue their own pleasure at any cost by refusing to submit to the dictates of the social law.[50] This psychoanalytic theory allows me to tie together the rise of Right-wing populism with the addiction to media technologies, the spread of consumer capitalism, and the medicalization of discontent.[51]

Caught between the Right-wing backlash against globalization and the Left-wing response, we find the centrist position, which often represents a politics of compromise and virtue signaling.[52] For instance, in the United States, centrist politicians in the Democratic Party recognize the real threat of climate change, but their solutions are usually partial gestures predicated on not upsetting the lifestyles of the upper-middle class professionals to which they cater.[53] These centrists want others to like them, and they have a great need to be seen as virtuous, but they do not base their policies on pure science, and they are unable to correct their failed efforts because they do not want to admit when they are wrong.[54] Although, they may show an awareness of global progress, they are afraid of celebrating it because they fear appearing insensitive to the less fortunate.

As I argued in my book *The Psychopathology of Political Ideologies*, it is necessary to distinguish among five different political belief systems, which are based on five different set of unconscious processes: conservative masochism, Left-wing hysteria, Right-wing borderline personality, centrist narcissism, and liberal neutrality.[55] From this perspective, liberal neutrality represents the foundation of modern globalization, while the other ideologies reveal different defenses against this political and psychological perspective.

In each of the following chapters, I will focus on particular ideological responses to globalization and psychoanalysis. What we will find is that the same individual and social forces resisting globalization and the need for a global government also resist psychoanalysis. The end result is that a clearer understanding of the theory and practice of Freudian psychoanalysis will help to establish how we defend and extend our shared global progress in the future.

Notes

1. Pinker, Steven. *Enlightenment Now: The Case for Reason, Science, Humanism, and Progress.* New York: Penguin, 2018.
2. Freud, Sigmund. "The Denial." *The Psychoanalytic Review (1913–1957)* 24 (1937): 420.
3. Samuels, Robert, and Robert Samuels. "The unconscious and the primary processes." *Freud for the Twenty-First Century: The Science of Everyday Life* (2019): 27–42.
4. Samuels, Robert, and Robert Samuels. "Logos, global justice, and the reality principle." *Zizek and the Rhetorical Unconscious: Global Politics, Philosophy, and Subjectivity*(2020): 65–86.

5. Cole, Alyson Manda. *The cult of true victimhood: From the war on welfare to the war on terror*. Stanford University Press, 2007.
6. Freud, Sigmund. *The future of an illusion*. Broadview Press, 2012.
7. Dobbelaere, Karel. *Secularization: An analysis at three levels*. Vol. 1. Peter Lang, 2002.
8. Walls, Gary B. "Toward a critical global psychoanalysis." *Psychoanalytic Dialogues* 14.5 (2004): 605–634.
9. Greene, Gayle. "The Myth of Neutrality, Again?." *Shakespeare Left and Right*. Routledge, 2015. 23–29.
10. Beck, Glenn. *The Great Reset: Joe Biden and the Rise of Twenty-First-Century Fascism*. Simon and Schuster, 2022.
11. Frank, Thomas. *Listen, Liberal: Or, what ever happened to the party of the people?*. Macmillan, 2016.
12. Stiglitz, Joseph E. *Globalization and its discontents revisited: Anti-globalization in the era of Trump*. WW Norton & Company, 2017.
13. Shermer, Michael. *The moral arc: How science and reason lead humanity toward truth, justice, and freedom*. Macmillan, 2015.
14. Pinker, Steven. *Enlightenment Now: The Case for Reason, Science, Humanism, and Progress*. New York: Penguin, 2018: 15.
15. Henderson, David R. "The Wonder of Modern Life." *Regulation* 41 (2018): 52.
16. Kim, Suehye. "Unpacking the international assessment data of literate population: The challenge and opportunity for global monitoring on adult literacy." *The SNU Journal of Education Research* 27 (2018): 29–45.
17. Kumar, Deepali, et al. "COVID-19: a global transplant perspective on successfully navigating a pandemic." *American Journal of Transplantation* 20.7 (2020): 1773–1779.
18. Henrich, Joseph. *The WEIRDest people in the world: How the West became psychologically peculiar and particularly prosperous*. Penguin UK, 2020.
19. Samuels, Robert. *The psychopathology of political ideologies*. Routledge, 2021.
20. Antonio, Robert J., and Douglas Kellner. "Communication, modernity, and democracy in Habermas and Dewey." *Symbolic Interaction* 15.3 (1992): 277–297.
21. Johnson, Steven. *Extra life: A short history of living longer*. Penguin, 2022.
22. Shermer, Michael. "The Rational Optimist: How Prosperity Evolves." *Nature* 466.7306 (2010): 564–565.
23. Pagden, Anthony. *The Enlightenment: and why it still matters*. Oxford University Press, 2013.
24. Descartes, René. *A discourse on method*. Aladdin Book Company, 1901.
25. Samuels, Robert, and Robert Samuels. "Logos, global justice, and the reality principle." *Zizek and the Rhetorical Unconscious: Global Politics, Philosophy, and Subjectivity*(2020): 65–86.

26. Boncardo, Robert. "Sixty years of Sartre's Critique: Revisiting The Critique of Dialectical Reason today." *Thesis Eleven* 161.1 (2020): 108–123.
27. Papastephanou, Marianna. "And that's not all:(Sur) faces of justice in philosophy of education." *Philosophies* 6.1 (2021): 10.
28. Rauch, Jonathan. *The constitution of knowledge: A defense of truth*. Brookings Institution Press, 2021.
29. McAdam, Doug. "Culture and social movements." *Culture and politics: A reader* (2000): 253–268.
30. Leider, Robert J. "Analytic neutrality—a historical review." *Psychoanalytic Inquiry* 3.4 (1983): 665–674.
31. Thompson, M. Guy. "Freud's conception of neutrality." *Contemporary Psychoanalysis* 32.1 (1996): 25–42.
32. Renik, Owen. "The perils of neutrality." *The Psychoanalytic Quarterly* 65.3 (1996): 495–517.
33. Freud, Sigmund. "Formulations Regarding the Two Principles in Mental Functioning." D. *Rapaport (Ed.), Organization and Pathology of Thought. Selected Sources, New York and London (Columbia University Press) 1951, pp. 315–328.*(1951).
34. Freud, Sigmund. "Mourning and melancholia." *The standard edition of the complete psychological works of Sigmund Freud*14.1914–1916 (1917): 237–258.
35. Robinson, William I. "Theories of globalization." *The Blackwell companion to globalization* (2007): 125–143.
36. Antonacopoulou, Elena P., and Yiannis Gabriel. "Emotion, learning and organizational change: Towards an integration of psychoanalytic and other perspectives." *Journal of Organizational Change Management* 14.5 (2001): 435–451.
37. Freud, Sigmund. "A child is being beaten." *The International Journal of Psycho-Analysis* 1 (1920): 371.
38. Freud, Sigmund, and Joseph Breuer. *Studies in hysteria*. Penguin, 2004.
39. Israëls, Han, and Morton Schatzman. "The seduction theory." *History of Psychiatry* 4.13 (1993): 23–59.
40. Freud, Sigmund. *Dora: An analysis of a case of hysteria*. Simon and Schuster, 1997.
41. Samuels, Robert, and Robert Samuels. "Victim politics: Psychoanalyzing the neoliberal conservative counter-revolution." *Psychoanalyzing the Left and Right after Donald Trump: Conservatism, Liberalism, and Neoliberal Populisms*(2016): 7–29.
42. Freud, Sigmund. *Group Psychology and the Analysis of the Ego*. Read Books Ltd., 2014.
43. Shapiro, Ruth B., and Constance L. Katz. "Fairy tales, splitting, and ego development." *Contemporary Psychoanalysis* 14.4 (1978): 591–602.

44. Masterson, James F., and Donald B. Rinsley. "The borderline syndrome: The role of the mother in the genesis and psychic structure of the borderline personality." *The International journal of psycho-analysis* 56 (1975): 163.
45. Neel, Jasper. *Aristotle's voice: Rhetoric, theory, and writing in America*. SIU Press, 1994.
46. Samuels, Robert, and Robert Samuels. "Pathos, Hysteria, and the Left." *Zizek and the Rhetorical Unconscious: Global Politics, Philosophy, and Subjectivity* (2020): 33–47.
47. Rodrik, Dani. "Why does globalization fuel populism? Economics, culture, and the rise of right-wing populism." *Annual Review of Economics* 13 (2021): 133–170.
48. Hayek, Friedrich August. *The road to serfdom: text and documents--the definitive edition*. Vol. 2. University of Chicago Press, 2009.
49. Samuels, Robert, and Robert Samuels. "Catharsis: The politics of enjoyment." *Zizek and the Rhetorical Unconscious: Global Politics, Philosophy, and Subjectivity* (2020): 7–31.
50. Freud, Sigmund. "The passing of the Oedipus complex." *The International Journal of Psycho-Analysis* 5 (1924): 419.
51. Levert, Natasha Petty. "A comparison of Christian and non-Christian males, authoritarianism, and their relationship to Internet pornography addiction/compulsion." *Sexual Addiction & Compulsivity* 14.2 (2007): 145–166.
52. Liu, Catherine. *Virtue hoarders: The case against the professional managerial class*. U of Minnesota Press, 2021.
53. Frank, Thomas. *Listen, Liberal: Or, what ever happened to the party of the people?*. Macmillan, 2016.
54. Samuels, Robert, and Robert Samuels. "Beyond Hillary Clinton: Obsessional Narcissism and the Failure of the Liberal Class." *Psychoanalyzing the Left and Right after Donald Trump: Conservatism, Liberalism, and Neoliberal Populisms* (2016): 31–59.
55. Samuels, Robert. *The psychopathology of political ideologies*. Routledge, 2021.

CHAPTER 2

The Future of an Illusion and the Conservative Rejection of Globalization

Abstract This chapter argues that psychoanalysis offers a unique perspective on nationalism and the conservative rejection of globalization. By examining Freud's *The Future of an Illusion*, we gain insight into how in order to understand the future, we must not only understand the past, but we also have to gain insight into the present. I argue that the move to global science, democracy, and capitalism is blocked by a set of psychological defense mechanisms defining conservative ideology. I will also use Freud's insights to posit that the only way we can reverse climate change is if we change our view of nature itself.

Keywords Freud • Climate change • Nature • Conservative ideology • *The Future of an Illusion* • Democracy • Science • Global politics • Reason • Truth

This chapter argues that psychoanalysis offers a unique perspective on nationalism and the conservative rejection of globalization. By examining Freud's *The Future of an Illusion*, we gain insight into how in order to understand the future, we must not only understand the past, but we also have to gain insight into the present.[1] We shall see the move to global science, democracy, and capitalism is blocked by a set of psychological defense mechanisms defining conservative ideology. I will also use Freud's insights to posit that the only way we can reverse climate change is if we change our view of nature itself.

Freud's Approach to Our Global Future

At the start of his text on the future of humankind, Freud articulates why it is so difficult to address global issues:

> Having lived for quite some time within a specific culture and tried repeatedly to study the nature of its origins and the path of its development, one also feels tempted just occasionally to turn and look in the other direction and ask what fate has in store for that culture and what changes it is destined to undergo. One quickly becomes aware, however, that any such venture is invalidated from the outset by several factors, chief among which is that only a few individuals are capable of commanding an overview of human activity in all its ramifications. Most people have found it necessary to concentrate on one or a small number of fields; yet the less a person knows about past and present, the shakier that person's judgement will inevitably be with regard to the future. (3)

This initial acceptance of our inability to comprehend the totality of human culture represents one of Freud's key Enlightenment values, which concerns an acceptance of the limits of our knowledge. Following Kant, Freud defines modern science in part by humility and the realization that we cannot know everything, and our understanding is limited by our perspective.[2] In fact, in *Totem and Taboo*, he argues that an essential difference between civilizations centered on religion and ones based on science is that in the scientific world, we give up a belief that we can know everything or that some higher power has complete knowledge.[3] Modern science, then, begins with an acknowledgement of lack and limitations. Yet, this lack of knowledge drives a desire to know the truth about reality.

The pursuit of the reality principle is centered on gaining a limited, impartial view of the world, but this project is itself blocked by individual psychology: "Another factor is that, in this judgement in particular, the subjective expectations of the individual play a role that is hard to assess; yet those expectations turn out to depend on purely personal elements in an individual's own experience, his or her more or less hopeful attitude to life, as dictated by temperament and by degree of success or lack of it" (6). Freud affirms here that one of the greatest obstacles for understanding the world is our own personality and particular psychopathology. In other words, as we shall see, particular ideologies cater to specific psychopathologies.[4]

From Freud's perspective, the only way to gain a more accurate sense of the world is for people to be able to remove themselves from their own thoughts, feelings, and judgments: "there is the effect of the remarkable fact that people in general experience their present almost naively, unable to appreciate what it holds; they must first put some distance between it and them—in other words, the present must first have become the past before it will furnish clues for assessing what is to come" (6). This need for distance and delay points to a central aspect of modernity, globalism, and the reality principle, which involves the ability of people to remove themselves from their own understanding.[5] Starting with his "Project for a Scientific Psychology," Freud bases his theory and method on the Enlightenment ideal of neutrality and free thought.[6] Just as the analyst has to refrain from judgment in order to help the patient to say whatever comes to their mind, the modern scientist is supposed to employ reason by removing all personal self-interest through the process of critical introspection.[7]

Of course, this goal of neutral reason can never be fully attained, but it shapes the modern global institutions of science and universal human rights. Freud's text, then, shows how in order to understand reason, you have to use reason, and this discourse of truth is difficult to achieve. Thus, the biggest resistance to understanding and pursuing global progress is our own resistances to reason itself.[8] In fact, one could argue that Freud's entire work is dedicated to applying reason to unreason so that more reason can be achieved.[9]

Freuds Definition of Human Society

Before Freud articulates how we can more effectively make the world more reasonable, he provides a very interesting definition of human societies: "It includes on the one hand all the knowledge and skill that humanity has acquired in order to control the forces of nature and obtain from it goods to satisfy human needs, and on the other hand all the institutions that are required to govern the relations of human beings one to another and in particular the distribution of such goods as can be obtained" (7). This understanding of human society focuses on the use of knowledge to control nature and to satisfy human needs by organizing the ways people interact and distribute goods. Using a functionalist theory, Freud posits that the main goal of civilization is to maintain stability by regulating nature and human relationships.[10] In many ways, this is a conservative model because the central task is to conserve the social order.[11]

In his description of the conservative foundation of human societies, Freud often sounds like a Marxist because he realizes that behind the quest for social stability, one finds the dual drives to achieve instinctual satisfaction and exploit others for profit:

> The two directions of culture are not independent of each other, firstly because the mutual relations of human beings are extensively influenced by the amount of drive-satisfaction made possible by the commodities available, secondly because the individual human being can himself, vis-à-vis another person, assume the relationship of a commodity in so far as that other person makes use of the said individual's labour or takes the individual as sexual object, but thirdly because every individual is, in virtual terms, an enemy of culture, which is in fast supposed to constitute a universal human interest. (7)

Freud combines psychoanalysis and Marxism here by arguing that societies not only have to try to satisfy human impulses, but they also function to turn people into commodities and sexual objects.[12] He adds that while society itself should be a universal value, every individual is actually an enemy of the state.

This battle between society and the individual cannot be resolved for Freud, and it is wrong to see him as promoting either individual liberation or social regulation; instead, throughout his career, he maintained that there is a fundamental, unresolvable conflict shaping human beings.[13] In fact, as we shall see in later chapters, the promise to resolve this conflict is often at the center of most ideologies; however, for Freud, we can never escape this primary conflict.[14] Moreover, Freud's conservative view of culture claims that the driving force behind civilization is conserving a social order dedicated to controlling nature and distributing goods: "Their purpose is not only to put in place a certain distribution of goods but also to maintain it; there is a need, in fact, for them to protect against the hostile impulses of humanity everything that serves to tame nature and generate commodities" (8). Freud's realism here points to the fact that behind every call for social order, we find an economic imperative, which also requires people giving up their own desires.

In one of his most critical insights, Freud affirms that conservative social orders are predicated on the ability of a powerful minority to impose their will on the disempowered masses: "This gives the impression that culture is something imposed on a reluctant majority by a minority that has managed to gain possession of the instruments of power and coercion" (8). From this perspective, civilization is defined by exploitation and coercion, and yet Freud also claims that social arrangements can be made less oppressive if they are based on the modern principles of equality and individual freedom, even if those ideals are never fully attained.

While Freud does at times point to ways of moving beyond conservative ideology and an oppressive social hierarchy, he never wavers from his fundamental argument that the conflict between individuals and society can never be resolved:

> One would think that some rearrangement of human relationships must be possible such as would cause the sources of dissatisfaction with culture to dry up by renouncing coercion and the suppression of drives and allowing people to devote themselves to acquiring and enjoying commodities undisturbed by inner discord. That would be the Golden Age, except that one wonders whether such a condition can ever be realized. It seems instead that every culture must be based on coercion and drive renunciation; it does not even appear certain that, with coercion removed, the majority of human beings will be prepared to take upon themselves the labour that must be performed if greater quantities of essential commodities are to be obtained. (8)

Freud is clearly not one to endorse pure individualism or the ability of humans to do away with an economic system based on commodities and enforced labor.[15] His tragic vision of humankind is honest and realistic, and this is why so many people from different ideological perspectives are quick to dismiss it.

Since Freud is dedicated to discovering the truth through free thought and critical introspection, he refuses to repress upsetting aspects of human life: "We need in my view to accept that destructive (i.e. anti-social and ant-cultural) tendencies are present in all human beings and that in a largest proportion of people such tendencies are powerful enough to dictate their behavior within human society" (8–9). Just as our knowledge is always limited, Freud asserts that our ability to control our anti-social impulses is also limited, and so we must build the future by recognizing these limitations.[16]

Although most Marxist analysts would focus on how best to distribute goods in society, Freud argues that this approach is not sufficient:

> Whereas our first impression was that the key thing about culture was the conquest of nature in order to obtain the commodities essential to life and that the dangers threatening culture could be removed by effective distribution of such goods among human beings, the emphasis now seems to have shifted away from the material towards the mental. It becomes crucial whether and to what extent the burden of the libidinal sacrifices imposed on human beings can be successfully lightened and human beings reconciled to and compensated for the part of that burden that inevitably remains. (9)

From this perspective, it is necessary to think beyond the social distribution of material goods so that one can address the problems caused by the social demands for instinctual sacrifice.[17] For Freud, a key factor to this analysis is the question of whether people think they are being properly compensated for what they are giving up.

Freud not only thinks that there will always be discontentment in civilization, but he also affirms that the majority of human beings will have to be forced to work and to give up their drives in order to make society function: "Domination of the mass by a minority can no more be dispensed with than coercion to perform cultural work, because masses are lethargic and unreasonable, they are averse to renouncing their drives, they cannot be persuaded by arguments that this is unavoidable, and individuals within masses reinforce one another in giving free rein to their lack of restraint" (9). This rather negative conception of human nature undermines the argument that people want to sacrifice for a shared goal and that they desire to work, and they are susceptible to reason. Yet, Freud's entire discourse is founded on applying reason to unreason, and so we have to ask how can a global society centered on rationality, science, and democracy be possible?[18]

Cultural Ideals and Narcissism

Before Freud articulates his vision of a more reason-based society, he articulates his theory of the ego ideal in relation to narcissism:

> the satisfaction that the ideal gives to those involved in a culture is narcissistic in nature, being based on pride in what has already been achieved. For it to be complete, it requires comparison with other culture that have

plumped for different achievement and evolved different ideals. On the strength of those differences, every culture gives itself the right to look down on the others. This is how culture ideals occasion rupture and hostility between different culture groups-most obviously amongst nations. (15–16)

Freud's important insight here is that nationalism is in part derived by the need for people to idealize their own state by comparing it to other less admired societies.[19] As Lacan articulates in his theory of the mirror stage and the structure of narcissism, the ego ideal represents the place from which people see themselves as loveable.[20] In his description of a paradigmatic scene, Lacan describes how a child will see itself in the mirror and then look back at a parent to see the parent's recognition and approval.[21] For Lacan, the subject wants his ideal ego to be verified by the ego ideal, and this unconscious psychological dynamic causes a double alienation since one conforms to what others value, and then one turns to others to have that conformity recognized.[22]

In terms of nationalism, the subject sees himself as belonging to a particular nation that is contrasted with other nations, and therefore, our sense of self and our pride in our nation are relative and alienating.[23] Freud adds that we are not only relying on comparing our nation to other less favorable nations, but internally, one group is compared to another group. This psychoanalytic social theory teaches us that identity is always based on difference, and the self is defined by the other.[24] Moreover, there is always a judgment of value shaping the internal and external hierarchy. Although it is clear that Freud believes this type of nationalism and classism is hard to avoid, we shall see how he later offers some possible alternatives.

For Freud, the narcissistic foundation of nationalism helps to convince the marginalized masses that their sacrifices for society are worthwhile: "Narcissistic satisfaction arising out of the cultural ideal is also one of the forces successfully countering cultural hostility within the culture group. Not only do the privileged classes, who enjoy the benefits of that culture, share in it; the oppressed may share in it, too, in that the right to despise outsiders is their compensation for the restrictions placed on them in their own circle" (16). The key idea here is that while people may be oppressed and looked down at in their own nation, they can always gain a sense of narcissistic pride by looking down at other countries and internal groups that are more despised.[25] Of course, it is this type of comparative judgment and narcissistic narcissism that often blocks the acceptance of a more globalized world. After all, if oppressed people cannot idealize their own nation and look down at other countries, then what is stopping them from rebelling against their own state?

I believe that Freud adds here an important contribution to our understanding of nationalism and the resistance to globalization and global government. Since identity is often formed and maintained through difference, how can a global world provide the same type of identification and stability? In other words, what is the true outside enemy of a global society?[26] Is destructive weather, the threat of pandemics, the spread of financial panic, or the threat of war enough to compensate people for their instinctual renunciations?

The Return of Nature

Interestingly, Freud claims that at the foundation of all human societies is a common enemy and that enemy is nature itself: "It was precisely because of the perils with which nature threatens that we got together in the first place and created culture, which is meant among other things to enable us to live together. Indeed, the main function of culture, the real reason for its existence, is to shield us against nature" (18–19). Since the main task of society is to control nature, we have to ask if the threat of climate change is enough to bring us all together in order to fight a common enemy?[27] This same question can be applied to biological pandemics, which also present nature as a threat to our existence. According to this logic, a key way to enhance global solidarity is to represent nature itself as the ultimate enemy. Therefore, instead of climate change activists seeking to gain support by idealizing nature, it might be more effective to demonize nature as the main enemy to rally around against.[28]

Freud's radical critique of nature offers a new alternative path for global solidarity because it does not make social unity and sacrifice dependent on attacking other cultures and social classes. In fact, Freud's anti-sentimental view seeks to pose nature as an unrelenting negative force:

> There are the elements, which appear to mock any kind of human constraint: earth, which heaves and splits open, burying all things human and all the works of humankind; which when in tumult swamps and drowns everything; storms, which blow everything away; there are diseases, which we have only recently come to recognize as attacks by other living creatures,

> and finally there is the painful riddle of death, against which no remedy has yet been found, nor probably ever will. These powers nature lines up against us, magnificent, cruel, relentless, reminding us of our weakness and of the helplessness we had thought our culture activities would overcome. (19)

For Freud, nature humbles us and teaches us that we cannot control everything.[29] Although many will be repulsed by the idea of debasing nature, Freud's discourse offers us an interesting path to global progress. Not only must we learn to despise external nature, but we also have to learn to be wary of our own inner nature.

Nature proves that our individual and social attempts to control the world will always fail, and so we must find some way to limit the effects of the Real.[30] Furthermore, Freud affirms that human solidarity is often triggered by a shared response to natural disasters: "One of the few pleasing and uplifting impressions furnished by the human race is when, faced with an elements disaster, it forgets its cultural muddle-headedness and all its internal problems and enmities and recalls the great common task of preserving itself against the superior might of nature" (19). Using this logic, we should use the threats caused by climate change and pandemics to enhance global solidarity and the need for a shared sacrifice to fight a common enemy.[31] It turns out that the mythical and mystical idealization of nature may be one of the biggest stumbling blocks to our need for a global enemy.

A Bad Consolation

Not only do we tend to idealize nature, but we also turn to culture in order to provide compensation for our instinctual renunciations:

> culture does not cease to operate once it has performed its task of defending the individual human against nature; it simply continues that task by other means. In this case, the task is a multiple one: man's badly threatened self-esteem craves consolation, the world and life need to lose their terror, and at the same time humanity's thirst for knowledge, which is of course driven by the strongest practical interest, craves an answer. With the first step, much is already gained. And that is to humanize nature. (20)

Instead of confronting the horrific nature of nature, humans seek to contain its threat through a process of anthropomorphism.[32] Since we do not want to be terrorized by the Real, and we do not want to admit that we cannot control it, our unconscious psychological strategy is to treat nature as if it is human.

In another brilliant move, Freud argues that what prevents us from accepting and confronting our natural enemy is the way we seek to perceive nature as a person:

> Impersonal forces and fates are unapproachable, they remain forever alien. But if passions rage in the elements as they do in the human heart, if even death is not something spontaneous but an act of violence perpetrated by a will, if everywhere in nature a person is surrounded by beings like those he knows from his own society, then he will breathe easier, feel at home in quite unfamiliar surroundings, be able, mentally, to deal with irrational fears; a person may still be defenceless but he is not helpless any longer, not paralysed, he can at least react. (20)

By translating nature into human aspects, the natural threats are reduced, and people become less threatened, but this process, that is often celebrated in poetry and the arts, turns out to be a bad thing since we need to fear nature in order to rally around fighting it.[33]

My argument here is not that we should get rid of natural preserves or start eliminating other species; rather, we have to take on a more realistic and truthful view of the natural world. We also need to use the threats posed by the environment and biological contagions to produce a global response centered on global solidarity.[34] By idealizing and anthropomorphizing nature, we end up removing the real threats it poses. Moreover, as Freud posits, this response to real natural threats often is the cause for shared delusions: "Similarly, a person does not simply turn the forces of nature into people among whom he is able to move as amongst his peers; that would not do justice, in fact, to the over powering impression he has of them. Instead, he invests them with a paternal character, turning them into gods, and in the process following not only an infantile model but also, as I have tried to show, a phylogenetic model" (21). In this theory of religion, Freud claims that the creation of a higher power is derived in part from our desire to translate nature into a human-like form. As a bridge between nature and humans, gods play the role of translating the unknowable Real into a shared cultural symbol.[35] Meanwhile, religion blocks global progress because it does not rely on scientific reason, and it mystifies our natural enemy.

Freud also critiques religion for the way that it provides a false psychological compensation for instinctual renunciation and social oppression: "The latter retain their triple function of warding off the terrors of nature, reconciling humans to the cruelty of fate, notably as revealed in death, and compensating them for the sufferings and privations imposed upon them by living together in a culture group" (21). Since everyone will die, and humans are the only animals that know they will die, one of the greatest threats that nature poses to humans is the fear of one's life ending, but this aspect of our mortality is hidden by the religious conception of the afterlife.[36] For Freud, a problem with this denial of death is that it takes away one of the only things that might motivate people to pursue science and a better social organization. If people are not fearful of dying because they will continue to live in an afterlife, they may lose their desire to fight nature and confront the reality of our world.

Freud adds that as societies develop and believe less in divine intervention, they begin to use religion to justify social norms and prohibitions:

> The task of the gods now becomes to make good the ills and shortcomings of culture, to heed the sufferings that people inflict on one another in living together, and to supervise implementation of the rules of culture with which humans find it so hard to comply. The rules of culture are themselves deemed to be of divine provenance; exalted above human society, they are extended to nature and world events. (17–18)

We should notice that for Freud, religion is not just about prohibitions since it also serves to compensate people on an imaginary level for their instinctual renunciations and for the suffering caused by human interaction.[37] In terms of global progress and the need to confront real threats like climate change, pandemics, war, and poverty, religious belief undermines these efforts since it either represses their existence, claims that a god will fix things, or provides some type of mental compensation.[38]

Of course, for Freud there is a parallel between the development of individuals and the development of societies, and this means that both begin with the state of the helpless subject in relation to a powerful caregiver: "In this way a treasury of ideas is created, born of the need to make human helplessness bearable, its building materials memories of everyone's own helplessness and that of the childhood of the human race" (18). The primal relation between the helpless child and the powerful Other is essential for Freud's theory of love, hypnosis, and the formation of social groups like the army, the church, and the political rally.[39] In all of these social situations, the human subject suspends all reality testing and morality as one submits to an idealized Other who has taken on the role of the sublime object of ideology.[40]

Freud's big move here is to argue that at its foundation, premodern society demands the total submission of the subject, and it is only with the invention of modernity that social subjectivity is combined with individual autonomy and critical thinking. As Kant struggles to articulate, the Enlightenment seeks to allow for social sacrifice and individual freedom at the same time.[41] Since Kant and Freud do not want to eliminate reason as the driving force behind modern science and democracy, they have to place in a dialectical relation, universal laws and the protection of individual rights. For instance, many modern constitutions seek to allow everyone the same rights of free political speech or the right vote or gather in groups.[42] The goal is to protect the individual and the group at the same time, and this requires combining universality and freedom together.

Instead of recognizing that human social institutions are always imperfect artificial constructions directed towards balancing the rights of the individual and the needs of the group, religions ascribe to an all-knowing higher power the role of "the superior wisdom that guides this process, the universal goodness that finds expression in it, the justice that finds implementation through it …" (19). This transference of responsibility from humans to a supernatural power often serves to prevent the solution to global problems and the formation of new human-made institutions.

Although it is clear that as the world becomes more modern and global, it also becomes more secular, there is still a great deal of resistance to globalization caused by the retention of religious belief.[43] However, even the most religious people still go to hospitals when they are sick and use science and technology to improve their lives. There is also a constant replacement of religious traditions and laws by secular institutions, even if this process is slow and uneven.[44] In fact, most of the shift from religion to science has occurred without any direct confrontation as people learn to rely on reason and democracy to ensure rights and longer lives. Furthermore, even though most people do not understand the source or even the evidence of global progress, they still profit from it, and yet, we need to understand the positive aspects of globalization so that we can continue to enhance what has worked in the past and stop what has prevented real progress.

As one of the major resistances to modern globalization, religion is often used to enhance nationalism and a sense of ethnic superiority:

With God now a single being, relations towards him could recover the intimacy and intensity of the child's relationship with its father. But having done so much for their father, folk wanted to be rewarded, they wanted at least to become the only beloved child, the chosen people. Many centuries later, a pious America claimed to be 'God's own country', and for one of the forms in which humans worship the deity that is indeed true. (19)

The combination of religion and nationalism continues to be one of the strongest obstacles for universal human rights and the fight against global threats since individual nations, like the United States, believe that they have been chosen by a higher power to be exceptional, and therefore they do not have to sacrifice their own particular interests for the interests of others.[45]

Freud shows himself to be keenly aware of the ways that religion harms our ability to confront our most pressing global issues: "But such as they are these ideas (religious in the broadest sense) are reckoned the most precious possession of culture, the most valuable thing it has to offer its participants, held in far higher esteem than all the skills of parting the earth from its treasures, feeding humanity, fending off disease, etc." (19–20). Freud's secular humanism helps him to see how destructive conservative ideology can be since the belief in a higher power undermines the fight against poverty, disease, and famine.[46] While many people on the Left, Right, and center want to cling to a respect for religious and ethnic identity, the founder of psychoanalysis does not subscribe to a relativistic perspective. As unfashionable as it is today, Freud affirms the need to make judgments concerning the comparative value and success of particular social systems.

As an Enlightenment thinker, what most repulses Freud about religion is the way that religious ideas are not the product of reason or empirical experimentation; instead, he critiques religious ideas because "they are dogmas, statements about facts and circumstances of external (or internal) reality that convey something we have not discovered for ourselves and that demand to be believed. Since they impart information about what is most important and most interesting for us in life, they are valued particularly highly" (24). As the developer of the methods of free association and analytic neutrality, Freud is against all dogmatic thinking and inherited belief.[47] Even though many see psychoanalysis as unscientific, Freud's work reveals that the foundation of modern science is the combination of impartiality and empirical reality.[48]

Following Descartes, Freud defines reason as the ability to distinguish truth from falsehood, and through his dedication to the reality principle and science, he declares: "There is no authority higher than reason" (28). As we shall see through this book, the driving force behind past and future global progress is reason since both science and democratic law are based on the impartial judgment of truth and the critical rejection of fiction.[49] What we need to deal with climate change, pandemics, poverty, and war are global public policies based on the impartial judgment of evidence.

Freud's commitment to reason and universality stems from his desire to counter purely subjective and dogmatic thought: "If the truth of religious teachings depends upon an inward experience attesting that truth, what about the many people who do not have so rare an experience? Everyone can be required to use the gift of reason that they possess, but an obligation that applies to all cannot be based on a motive that exists only for very few" (28). In contrast to religious dogma, Freud posits that reason is available to all and is not centered on self-interest or a particular cultural bias.[50] This universal perspective is at the foundation of globalization centered on unbiased science and equal rights.

Although most people equate globalization with capitalism as a shared system of economic value, modernity relies on science and democratic law to regulate and limit the influence of capital accumulation.[51] Since science and the law are supposed to be impartial and universal, they should not be tainted by wealth and the pursuit of personal profit. Yet, as we shall see in the next chapter, this containment of global capitalism represents one of the biggest challenges for both the theory and practice of global progress. However, I argue that instead of simply dismissing the positive role economic development plays in globalism, we need to determine how to balance science and democracy with capitalism. Unfortunately, as we shall see, many on the Left reject both psychoanalysis and globalization because they do not understand the role played by neutrality in science, democracy, and analysis.

Notes

1. Sigmund Freud. The Future of an Illusion (p. 6). Penguin Books. Kindle Edition.
2. Horgan, John. *The end of science: Facing the limits of knowledge in the twilight of the scientific age*. Basic Books, 2015.
3. Freud, Sigmund. *Totem and taboo*. Phoemixx Classics Ebooks, 2021.

4. Samuels, Robert. *The psychopathology of political ideologies*. Routledge, 2021.
5. Freud, Sigmund. "Formulations on the two principles of mental functioning." *Unconscious phantasy*. Routledge, 2018. 67–76.
6. Freud, Sigmund, Marie Ed Bonaparte, Anna Ed Freud, Ernst Ed Kris, Eric Trans Mosbacher, and James Trans Strachey. "Project for a scientific psychology." (1954).
7. Lacey, Hugh. "Rehabilitating neutrality." *Philosophical studies*163 (2013): 77–83.
8. Rensmann, Lars. *The politics of unreason: The Frankfurt School and the origins of modern antisemitism*. Suny Press, 2017.
9. Levine, Donald N. "Freud, Weber, and modern rationales of conscience." *Emotions & Behavior Monographs* (1984).
10. Ormerod, Richard. "The history and ideas of sociological functionalism: Talcott Parsons, modern sociological theory, and the relevance for OR." *Journal of the Operational Research Society* 71.12 (2020): 1873–1899.
11. Morin, Olivier. "Cultural conservatism." *Journal of Cognition and Culture* 22.5 (2022): 406–420.
12. Althusser, Louis, and Warren Montag. "On Marx and Freud." *Rethinking Marxism* 4.1 (1991): 17–30.
13. Lacan, Jacques. *The ethics of psychoanalysis 1959–1960: The seminar of Jacques Lacan*. Routledge, 2013.
14. Freud, Sigmund. *Civilization and its discontents*. Broadview Press, 2015.
15. Roazen, Paul. *Freud: Political and social thought*. Transaction Publishers, 1970.
16. Rieff, Philip. *Freud: The mind of the moralist*. University of Chicago Press, 1979.
17. Marcuse, Herbert. *Eros and civilization: A philosophical inquiry into Freud*. Vol. 496. Beacon Press, 1974.
18. Heinrich, Joseph. "The weirdest people in the world: how the West became psychologically peculiar and particularly prosperous." *Farrar, Straus & Giroux* (2020).
19. Pick, Daniel. ""Freud's" Group Psychology" and the History of the Crowd." *History Workshop Journal*. No. 40. Oxford University Press, 1995.
20. Lacan, Jacques. *Four fundamental concepts of psychoanalysis*. Vol. 11. WW Norton & Company, 1998.
21. Pluth, Ed. "Remarks on Daniel Lagache's Presentation:"Psychoanalysis and Personality Structure"." *Reading Lacan's Écrits: From 'The Freudian Thing' to 'Remarks on Daniel Lagache'*. Routledge, 2019. 254–288.
22. Lacan, Jacques. "The Mirror Stage as Formative of the Function of the I as Revealed in Psychoanalytic Experience1." *Reading French Psychoanalysis*. Routledge, 2014. 97–104.

23. Cichocka, Aleksandra, and Aleksandra Cislak. "Nationalism as collective narcissism." *Current Opinion in Behavioral Sciences* 34 (2020): 69–74.
24. Quinn, Michael L. "Relative identity and ideal art: the Pirandello conflict and its political analogy." *Journal of Dramatic Theory and Criticism* (1989): 73–86.
25. Gaztambide, Daniel José. *A people's history of psychoanalysis: From Freud to liberation psychology*. Lexington Books, 2019.
26. Žižek, Slavoj. *A left that dares to speak its name: 34 untimely interventions*. John Wiley & Sons, 2020.
27. Klein, Naomi. *This changes everything: Capitalism vs. the climate*. Simon and Schuster, 2015.
28. Zizek, Slavoj. *Living in the end times*. Verso Books, 2011.
29. Barron, James, W., et al. "Sigmund Freud: The secrets of nature and the nature of secrets." *International Review of Psycho-Analysis* 18 (1991): 143–163.
30. Zupančič, Alenka. *Ethics of the real: Kant, Lacan*. Verso, 2000.
31. Juncker, Jean-Claude. "State of the Union 2015: Time for honesty, unity and solidarity." *European Commission* 9 (2015): 25.
32. Smith, David Livingstone. "Animism, realism and anti-realism." *Freud's Philosophy of the Unconscious*. Dordrecht: Springer Netherlands, 1999. 102–111.
33. Kracher, Alfred. "Imposing order—The varieties of anthropomorphism." *Studies in Science and Theology* 8 (2002): 239–261.
34. Greer, Scott L. "National, European, and global solidarity: COVID-19, public health, vaccines." *Eurohealth* 26.2 (2020): 104–108.
35. Ziebertz, Hans-Georg, ed. *The human image of God*. Brill, 2001.
36. Mellor, Philip A., and Chris Shilling. "Modernity, self-identity and the sequestration of death." *Sociology* 27.3 (1993): 411–431.
37. Mellor, Philip A., and Chris Shilling. "Modernity, self-identity and the sequestration of death." *Sociology* 27.3 (1993): 411–431.
38. Jenkins, Willis, Evan Berry, and Luke Beck Kreider. "Religion and climate change." *Annual review of environment and resources* 43 (2018): 85–108.
39. Freud, Sigmund. *Group Psychology and the Analysis of the Ego*. Read Books Ltd., 2014.
40. Zizek, Slavoj. *The sublime object of ideology*. Verso Books, 2019.
41. Wp10605ms!
42. Brennan Jr., William J. "The Bill of Rights and the states: The revival of state constitutions as guardians of individual rights." *NyuL rev.* 61 (1986): 535.
43. Liwerant, Judit Bokser. "Globalization, Secularization and Collective Identities: Encounters and Dilemmas of Multiple Modernities." *ProtoSociology* 38 (2021): 137–171.

44. Alvey, James E. "Economics and religion: Globalization as the cause of secularization as viewed by Adam Smith." *International Journal of Social Economics* (2005).
45. Brubaker, Rogers. "Religion and nationalism: Four approaches." *Nations and nationalism* 18.1 (2012): 2–20.
46. Smith, M. Brewster. "Humanistic psychology." *Journal of humanistic psychology* 30.4 (1990): 6–21.
47. Gay, Peter. *A godless Jew: Freud, atheism, and the making of psychoanalysis.* Yale University Press, 1987.
48. Samuels, Robert, and Robert Samuels. "Science and the reality principle." *Freud for the Twenty-First Century: The Science of Everyday Life* (2019): 5–16.
49. Spragens, Thomas A. *Reason and democracy.* Duke University Press, 1990.
50. Strenger, Carlo. "Freud, Jewish Universalism, and the Critique of Religion." *Psychoanalysis and Theism: Critical Reflections on the Grünbaum Thesis* (2010): 99.
51. Wagner, Peter. *Modernity.* Polity, 2012.

CHAPTER 3

The Left's Critique of Psychoanalysis and Globalization

Abstract Many have argued that psychoanalysis is not appropriate for the study of globalization and global politics because it is tied to an old, biased European Ideology and culture. Instead of seeing psychoanalysis as a universal discourse centered on the dialectical relationship between individuals and societies, critics assume that Freud's discourse is limited by being the product of the European Enlightenment. From this relativistic perspective, the need to respect all cultures undermines the ability of psychoanalysis to relate to global issues. However, this argument misses the way the analytic neutrality requires a suspension of personal and cultural bias, and this call for neutrality is also foundational for universal human rights and fact-based public policy.

Keywords Globalization • Global politics • Enlightenment • Freud • Neutrality • Science • Human rights • Universality • Public policy

Many have argued that psychoanalysis is not appropriate for the study of globalization and global politics because it is tied to an old, biased European Ideology and culture. For example, Gary B. Walls argues that, "psychoanalysis emerged in a specifically Western tradition of intellectual and social values. It is based on a philosophy of liberal individualism and thus has proved to be a therapeutic technique exhibiting constraints that have limited its applicability across cultures and classes" (606).[1] Instead of seeing psychoanalysis as a universal discourse centered on the dialectical relationship between individuals and societies, Walls makes the common assumption that Freud's discourse is limited by being the product of the European Enlightenment.[2] From this relativistic perspective, the need to respect all cultures undermines the ability of psychoanalysis to relate to global issues. However, what Walls' argument misses is the way the analytic neutrality requires a suspension of personal and cultural bias, and this call for neutrality is also foundational for universal human rights and fact-based public policy.[3]

With the global spread of modern democracy, science, and capitalism, a universal perspective with a universal subject has to be established, and psychoanalysis is the philosophy that best fits this globalizing culture.[4] As a bias against bias, modern science and democracy are based on the necessary but impossible ideals of equality and impartiality.[5] In turn, these ideals counter national, ethnic, and religious cultures and traditions. Thus, the centrist liberal desire to not offend any group and be seen as tolerant actually functions to block progress and justice.[6] In fact, one of the biggest resistances to globalization is the idea that since there is no common, agreed-upon set of values, then it is impossible to even define what progress might look like.[7] In order to counter this view, I have argued that most people can agree that the expansion of human lifespans is a foundational good, and so there is a shared value that we can use to judge different past and present cultures.

Another criticism that Walls voices is that psychoanalysis is both elitist and conformist: "Even in the context of Western culture, psychoanalysis has often been a socially conservative rather than a progressive force (Jacoby, 1983), operating with aims that were implicitly adaptive to the values of the dominant sectors of our own society and of limited or no value to oppressed, marginalized, or excluded members of society" (606). Although, it is clear that many practitioners of psychoanalysis have transformed the practice and theory into a model of adaptation, Freud's original method did not take sides in the fundamental conflict between society and the individual.[8] Moreover, the practice of free association is open to discussing any and all issues, and so it is hard to see it as restricted by a particular ideology or culture.[9] Freud was also against making psychoanalysis part of medicine in part to guard against the way that it has become an elitist profession.

As a discipline that challenges all identifications and identities, psychoanalysis can be seen as global because it has no inherent content.[10] From this perspective, it should be equally open to the marginalized and the privileged, but a certain Leftist tendency wants to discredit psychoanalysis because of its roots in the European Enlightenment.[11] From an extreme Left-wing perspective, any discipline that is not solely focused on issues of race, class, or gender is by definition exclusionary.[12] Yet, in a globalized world, what we need is a discourse that can be open to people from all different social groups. Since Walls and some other Left-leaning critics want to demonize psychoanalysis for its elitist cultural roots, the tendency is to present analysis as a replication of colonialist patriarchy: "In the spirit of its time, traditional psychoanalysis consisted of an authoritarian analyst–patient relationship and promulgated values such as a scientific approach to human affairs, the affirmation of paternalistic gender roles, individual achievement, personal responsibility, and a strongly bounded self" (606). Not only does Walls want to reject modern liberal individualism, but he also seeks to discredit science itself.[13] Here, we see how a relativistic perspective ends up denying the very things that make global progress possible. After all, is the value of medicine being rejected here because it has been developed in a particular cultural context by a specific group of people?

The Leftist critique of psychoanalysis is shown here to dovetail with the critique of globalization and the true causes of global progress. As an elitist academic discourse, this form of Left-wing hysteria is so bent on demonizing the Other that it is blind to how its own arguments undermine the ability of the marginalized and the poor to use science, capitalism, and democracy to improve their lives.[14] I call this discourse hysterical because it uses hyperbole, splitting, and repression to set up a clear, dramatic distinction between the good "Us" and the evil "Them." There is also a lack of awareness of its own aggression as it sees violence and oppression only coming from the Other as the self remains innocent and pure.[15]

When I have taught my undergraduate students who are Global Studies majors, I often find that they have internalized an extreme anti-globalism ideology. In one particular class, a student told me that she would leave the course for good if I did not announce to the other students that capitalism is inherently evil. While this may have been an extreme event, it does point to the lack of nuance and complexity in the Leftist critique of global capitalism. To be clear, I do not shy away from pointing to many of the negative effects of our current economic model, but it is also important to understand how many people have escaped dire poverty since the spread of modern capitalism. Unfortunately, too many professors and students only focus on the negative, and so they see the world from a depressive fantasy-frame. In other terms, by focusing on the negative aspects of globalization, capitalism, and psychoanalysis, they are able to find meaning, identity, and identification through suffering.[16] People also use their victim identifications to escape their own guilt and shame as they retain a sense of being pure and innocent, while evil is located outside of the self.[17]

Psychoanalysis Against the Particular

Returning to Walls critique of psychoanalysis, he argues that since psychoanalysis is based on a theory of universal human nature, it cannot help dismissing and devaluing particular cultures:

> The intellectual program of the Enlightenment had, since Bacon, sought to portray humankind as a part of nature and therefore subject to universal and invariant natural laws of the kind Newton discovered and that gave order to the physical universe. Although this viewpoint made possible the establishment of the scientific study of vast domains of human life that had previously been left to theology or speculative philosophy, it also had some unfortunate consequences on the understanding of the empirical diversity found among people around the world. (606)

It should be clear to anyone who has ever read Freud that his theory is not driven by biology or a universal human nature: At its foundation, psychoanalysis concerns the conflicts among particular societies, specific individuals, biological aspects, and real necessities.[18] It is absurd to compare his work to Newton's universal, invariant natural laws, but this false reading helps to make psychoanalysis and globalism look bad due to their supposed lack of recognizing diversity. Although it is true that Freud did privilege scientific societies over animistic and religious ones, he did not dismiss the rich, diversity of human cultures.[19]

One challenge that psychoanalysis and globalism face is this problem of how do you promote universalizing science, democracy, and capitalism without appearing to erase all cultural and individual differences. However, it should be clear that the best way to protect individual rights and freedoms is to apply shared laws and rules within a democratic system.[20] It should also be evident that the best way to help all people is to use science to improve medicine and health standards for everyone. Yet, there is a tendency on the Left to dismiss all of these positive aspects of modernity so that the focus can be placed on suffering and exploitation.

Another aspect of the Leftist critique of psychoanalysis and globalization is the argument that both discourses deny the importance of local and traditional practices and beliefs:

> Geertz (1973) argues that the Enlightenment view of human nature placed such an overbearing emphasis on universal characteristics that it relegated the differential effects of culture to secondary status. This approach denies to cultural beliefs, values, customs, language, and participation in social institutions their status as fundamental, irreducible elements of what makes us human. The cultural dimension is thereby often dismissed as a mere overlay of what is truly human. Stripped of its social contexts, human nature is ineluctably individualistic. (606–607)

Although psychoanalysis has often been accused of focusing on the isolated individual and ignoring larger social and cultural issues, Freud affirmed that the ego is caught between the demands of the social order (the super-ego), biological urges (the id), reality, and its own fight for survival.[21] Moreover, his theory of the ego ideal relates to how the ego judges itself in relation to cultural ideals and values.[22] To argue that Freud simply removes culture and the social is simply a misreading of the facts.[23]

Freud and Social Darwinism

One reason why Walls misreads and rejects Freud is that he misunderstands the basic theory of evolution: "Freud's thinking was also influenced by Darwin's theory of evolution, which emphasized individual organisms' competitive struggle for survival. In traditional evolutionary theory, species survival is dependent not on the organization of the group, but on the differential success of particular organisms in surviving and reproducing their genetic code" (607). Like so many others, Walls confuses individual self-preservation with the replication of genetic material.[24] According to evolutionary logic, survival of the fittest does not mean that individuals are rewarded for outcompeting each other; rather, survival is on the species level and has to do with the rate of reproduction of particular genetic codes. By confusing the competition between individuals with genetic survival, Walls seeks to attack Freud for ascribing to a biological determinism bent on selfish competition. The only way that he can make this claim is if he imposes his own misunderstandings onto Freud and Darwin, and one reason why he might be doing this is that he is driven to demonize these leading modern theories so that he can condemn science and modernity.[25]

The Left-wing critique of science, psychoanalysis, and evolutionary theory is often centered on the idea that Freud based his system on a mode of scientific racism, which is also used to justify inequality and exploitation on a global level[26]:

> Social Darwinism was a philosophy developed at the end of the 19th century, which extended Darwin's notion of the survival of the fittest to the realm of social theory. It assumed that competitive social, economic, and political struggles among individuals, races, and societies operated according to the same principles as Darwin's theory of the evolution of species. It expressed the idea that some individuals, social classes, races, and societies are inherently superior to others and therefore prevail in human affairs. This philosophy was often used as a moral justification for the European domination of non-Western people, and in our own society, for the domination of the so-called lower classes by the higher. (609)

One of the problems with this argument is that it disregards the long history of social hierarchy predating modern capitalism.[27] In fact, it is only after the start of the modern mode of economic exchange that we have seen an increase in human lifespans and an extension of rights to a wide-range of people.[28] Once again, the idea here is not to dismiss the destructive aspects of capitalism; instead, we have to look at the past and present from a neutral perspective. However, this call for impartiality is not possible for Left-wing critics who belief that there is no such thing as an unbiased perspective.[29] At times, this rejection of neutrality serves the purpose of supporting their own highly biased views.

I want to stress here that I am focusing on Walls' analysis, but many others share his perspective on psychoanalysis and globalization.[30] One reason why it is beneficial to look at his text is that he clearly combines a critique of psychoanalysis with a critique of globalism. For instance, in the following passage, he continues to associate Freud with a universal mode of social Darwinism: "Although social Darwinism was a purported extension of Darwin's theory from the biological to the social level of analysis,

Freud's (1913) theory of the neuroses could be seen as extending these principles of conflict and survival to the psychological level" (609). The problem with positing that Freud applied social Darwinism to individual psychology is that Freud often emphasized the ways people undermine their own self-interest.[31] Furthermore, neurosis is based on repression, and repression represents the ways people lie to themselves—so it is hard to see how Freud simply applies an evolutionary theory to individual subjectivity.[32]

Walls interpretation of globalization and psychoanalysis reveals how so much of the academic Left's understanding of the past and present world is determined by a small set of predetermined interpretations that are simply projected onto material with little complexity or reality testing.[33] One of my fears is that many students have internalized this perspective, and so they are unable to see many of the benefits of globalization and psychoanalysis. In fact, when I teach my global politics course, I often hear students repeat claims similar to the following from Walls: "At the beginning of the new millennium, globalized rather than nationalized forms of social organization are superceding traditional Western colonialism" (609). The argument here is that globalization is simply a new form of colonialism divorced from its former foundation in national imperialism; in other words, people are being colonized without the colonialists.[34] It is then capitalism itself that is represented as a vague global force invading all countries and reshaping their social structures.

Perhaps the most common complaint regarding globalization is that is will undermine all particular cultures from the inside and the outside:

> One of the problems is that many aspects of the functioning of traditional cultures are not compatible with the organization of a worldwide free market system, and so globalization contains opposing forces. Some of these forces recognize the importance of cultural diversity, and others tend toward a homogenization of world society in the service of a more efficient, expansive market society. (608)

On one level, this fear of lost traditions is realistic since one of the driving forces behind modern globalism is the replacement of religion with science.[35] There is also the modern drive to substitute democracy for traditional authorities as feudal social hierarchies are subverted by economic and geographical mobility. What we must ask the defenders of traditional cultures is if they think it is best for people to live without medicine or to be mired in dire poverty? The sentimental idealization of traditional, premodern societies is often based on a patronizing mode of racism where comfortable elites romanticize oppressed and exploited people.[36]

Against Liberal Democracy

Left-wing racism can be located in the way that critics dismiss the importance of individual rights and freedom for people who have never had the opportunity to escape dire poverty or oppressive social hierarchies.[37] Walls displays this attitude in the following passage:

> Liberal individualism emphasizes the value of freedom of the individual conceived in terms of inalienable rights, such as those guaranteed in the U.S. Constitution. This view gives individual needs ontological priority over social relationships. Like traditional psychoanalysis, such a view assumes a divergence between the needs of the individual and the requirements of society, and attempts to resolve conflicts in favor of the preservation of individual freedom. (608)

The first problem with this analysis is that it denies the importance of individual rights and freedom, and the second issue is that it fails to see how in modern democratic law, individual protections are grounded in equality and shared responsibility.[38] What is often misunderstood is that at the heart of modern liberal democracy is the dialectical relation between universal equality and individual freedom; thus, the way that individuals are protected is by giving them equal access to the law, which requires a judge treating everyone the same.[39] The preservation of individual freedom then requires a social contract centered on neutrality and universality.

For Walls, psychoanalysis and modern liberalism replace the social with the individual, and so they are easily dismissed as being anti-social. Moreover, Walls adds that the type of rights provided by liberal democratic law are empty abstractions:

> One problem with this view stems from the fact that liberal individualism conceives freedom and individuality primarily in terms of abstractions. The possibility that the actual administration of liberal individualism has differential effects on particular genders, races, or classes of individuals is hidden from view. It is hidden because the discourses on freedom within liberal individualism are defined in terms of universal rights administered by the universal procedures of a representative democracy (e.g., the Bill of Rights,

legal rights enforced by jury or bench trial, bureaucracies run by rules and regulations), and not in terms of specific relational obligations (e.g., the obligation to help a neighbor or to care for an aging parent).

Here the criticism of psychoanalysis and globalization is based on the notion that modern democratic law seeks to treat everyone the same regardless of race, class, or gender.[40] It is then universal equality itself that is rejected since the new goal is to focus on the rights of distinct group identities and circumstances. This now-common Left-wing criticism of modern democratic law appears to reject the very foundations of liberal democracy and universal human rights.[41]

While it is evident that our modern legal systems can be biased and ineffective, these failures are judged against the ideals of the system. If we affirm that the goals of universality and impartiality are necessary but impossible, the idea is to constantly strive to attain these ideals.[42] However, some argue that universality and impartiality are fake principles produced by the privileged in order to trick the marginalized.[43] Yet, we have seen a continuous expansion of rights covering new groups, and these minority-based social movements may begin by stressing their separate identity, but they are driven by the desire to be included into a system of universal human rights.[44] The problem with some Leftist criticisms of modern liberal democratic law is that they focus so much on the failures of the system that they refuse to accept the foundational ideals.

Rejecting Neutrality

It is interesting to note that the same rejection of global universality is applied to psychoanalytic neutrality.[45] In both cases, the argument is that the attempt to suspend all bias is a false way to protect privileges and disregard important differences and inequalites.[46] The problem with this perspective is that without the ideal of neutrality, you cannot have psychoanalysis, science, or democratic law. Although the desire to give special attention to particular cultural differences may be driven by good intentions, it ends up undermining the very things that help people live longer, freer, and more flourishing lives. For example, when people argue that we should respect all religious beliefs, does that mean that we should support a religion that discriminates against females or refuses to give life-saving medicine to children? Of course, this is a very difficult question, but modern liberal democracies allow for a freedom of belief unless those beliefs cause direct harm.

Walls' Left-wing criticism of global law, psychoanalysis, science, and capitalism revolves around the same issue of how do we treat individuals from a global, universalistic perspective: "Such a viewpoint relies on a generalized notion of interchangeable individuals that erases or regards as inconsequential the differences between individuals due to class, race, age, gender. The individual, not the system, is viewed as responsible for any unequal outcomes in a liberal society based on institutions of procedural justice" (608). What Walls appears to reject here is the very notion of an impersonal, universal subject, and it is this form of subjectivity that is essential for modern science, democracy, and psychoanalysis.[47] For instance, we want our scientists to judge empirical evidence without bias or self-interest, just as we want judges to base their decisions on the facts alone. From this perspective, universality, globalization, neutrality, objectivity, and equality are different names for the same thing. Humans have produced an artificial ideal perspective centered on the suspension of identity and identification, and it is this perspective that shapes our vital modern social institutions.[48] When people fail to understand and protect this ideal, they undermine the future of our global progress.

On the positive side, Walls is correct to tie the impersonal, universal perspective to psychoanalysis:

> Reflecting the cultural context of its origin, traditional psychoanalysis makes similar assumptions regarding the primacy of the individual in its theory—for example, in its assumption that the causes of neurosis are contained in the intrapsychic dynamics of the individual rather than the consequences of societal arrangements. Furthermore, psychoanalysts have assumed that individual differences can be subsumed under the fixed, universalizing procedures of the psychoanalytic situation.

What Walls misses in this discussion of the universal nature of psychoanalysis is the key idea that the non-judgment of the analyst allows for the free association of the patient. The reason, then, why the race, class, and gender of the analyst and the patient should not matter is that all identities and identifications should be called into question.[49] The subject of psychoanalysis is therefore universal and undetermined.

One possible reason why Walls refuses to accept any form of universality is that he sees a hidden destructive force of capitalism behind every modern, global institution and relation: "A second problem with this view is that Western society has combined liberal individualism with capitalism. Unfortunately, at times the humanistic values underlying liberal individualism conflict with the even more abstract and impersonal economic requirements of capitalism" (609). What is interesting is that the abstract and impersonal nature of capitalism is exactly what Marx found to be its major benefit.[50] For Marx, old feudal and patriarchal hierarchies and values were undermined by the capitalist exchange value, and this was a good thing because it allowed people to escape from an oppressive social order. From this perspective, capitalism served the historical function of modernizing the world by allowing for economic and geographic mobility.[51] Since the exchange value puts a price on everything and anything, every person and object is submitted to the same universal system. Although there are certainly negative aspects of this universality, it provides the driving force behind modernization and the extension of human lifespans.

Since many Leftist scholars and activists want to blame capitalism for all of the world's problems, they are unable to see the positive aspects of this economic system, and one of the results of this one-sided perspective is that the path out of dire poverty is removed from the people who most need it.[52] As global statistics show, modern capitalism is the first and only economic system that has been able to pull billions of people out of dire poverty, which has contributed to the extension of human lifespans.[53] In fact, throughout much of human history, societies have been highly unequal as exploitation is usually justified through a system of prejudices and stereotypes. Clearly, modern capitalism did not invent racism or sexism, yet, critics on the Left often claim that this economic order is the cause for all social evils.[54] In fact, for Walls, the driving force behind globalization is not liberal democracy; instead, he insists that the promotion of individual rights and freedoms is a cover for capitalistic expansion: "Although globalization is promoted as the spread of the humanistic philosophies of democracy and liberal individualism, the driving engine is actually the expansion of the economic system of capitalism" (609). By subsuming modern democracy under the banner of global capitalism, he follows the Leftist tradition of privileging economic determinism over culture and individual psychology.[55] One of the problems with this interpretation is that does not leave space for the contentious conflict between money and democratic politics. On the one hand, it would be wrong to hide the fact that wealthy people often control political institutions, and yet on the other hand, part of modernity involves the desire to separate democratic institutions from economic influence.[56]

As a necessary but impossible ideal, the goal of basing political and legal decision on the unbiased judgment of empirical facts requires the creation of laws seeking to regulate the roles money plays in politics. It is also necessary for governments to shape markets and help support economic activity, and yet, for a Left-wing critic like Walls, capitalism is purely a system of oppression: "If it were generally recognized that capitalism is a system of dominance and exploitation that requires the enrichment of the few and the relative impoverishment and subjugation of the vast majority, it would lead to the delegitimization and eventual collapse of the system. So the harsh terms of capitalist society are hidden behind the more acceptable moral ideologies of democracy and liberal individualism" (610). As I have been arguing, this one-sided critique of global capital erases the true history of economic development around the world.

Analysis Against Psychoanalysis

Coupled with the radical critique of economic globalization, we also find a shared rejection of psychoanalysis: "Critics have accused psychoanalysis of being a bourgeois science that serves as an agent of social conformity by medicalizing emotional suffering and diverting attention from the economic and political causes of psychological distress (Kovel, 1980). In other words, psychoanalysis has been accused of legitimizing the capitalist system when it results in emotional casualties manifested at the level of individual personality" (611). As I argued above, this understanding of psychoanalysis refuses to affirm the central role that neutrality plays for both the analyst and the patient: Since every topic is and should be allowed, it is hard to understand how it can be merely a practice of conformity.[57] However, it is true that many forms of analysis and therapy now seek to medicalize human suffering and repress the social contributions to individual symptoms, but I would argue that these modes of treatment go against the fundamental foundations of psychoanalysis itself.[58]

Walls is partially correct when he claims that there is a tendency to only provide psychoanalysis for the most affluent members of society:

> Psychoanalysis has been characterized as a therapy for educated, affluent, white, middle- or upper-class people from Western industrialized cultures. It is not for the poor, for people of color, or for people of non-Western, non-

industrialized cultures. Furthermore, psychoanalysis has been criticized for being profoundly patriarchal and sexist (see Flax, 1990). In practice, it has proved to be far from universally applicable or scientifically neutral. (611)

This rejection of the scientific foundation of psychoanalysis is coupled with a failure to see its universal nature. Although it is true that many psychoanalysts cater to the wealthy, there is nothing inherent in the practice or theory requiring this form of economic discrimination. Once again, my main argument against this Left-wing perspective is that it misrepresents psychoanalysis and globalization due to the same failure to accept the key ideal of neutrality. Just as global modern law and science require an impartial judge of empirical data, psychoanalysis is centered on the patient and the analyst taking on a neutral and universal perspective. In order to free associate, one must suspend judgment, and this removal of judgment is motivated by the analyst's refusal to judge. Once this core concept of neutrality is lost, we cannot understand psychoanalysis or modern globalization.

Zizek's Empty Subject

To further clarify this connection between psychoanalytic neutrality and globalization, I want to examine Slavoj Zizek's theory of the universal empty subject of modernity. One of Zzizek's central claim is that at the heart of the modern Enlightenment, we find Descartes' theory of the cogito ("I think"), which is defined as an empty, universal subject: "This purely formal-negative self-identity is the core of the Cartesian cogito …" (727).[59] Drawing from Lacan's idea that psychoanalysis can only start after Descartes' conception of the modern subject of science, Zizek affirms that the subject of psychoanalysis is empty of all content, and therefore this universal being is not defined by race, class, ethnicity or gender.[60]

Zizek combines this philosophical notion of universality with Marx's notion that on the level of the capitalist exchange value, all past, stable identities are melted away.[61] In other terms, the subject of modern capitalism is also empty and universal, and it is Zizek's argument that Marx himself gets his notion of universality from Hegel.[62] As the main philosopher of universality, Hegel helps us to see how this necessary but impossible ideal is always a work in progress. In other terms, we never have complete equality or neutrality, but we strive to attain this human ideal.

As I will argue in the next chapter, universal neutrality is often rejected not only by the Left but also by the Right, and this refusal to understand the modern universal empty subject represents a key aspect of the misunderstanding of globalization. Since the only way to have universal human rights is to treat everyone as if they are the same, the goals of impartiality and equality have to rely on necessary but impossible ideals. Likewise, psychoanalysis itself can only function if the analyst and patient take on the attitude of neutral, empty subjects open to whatever comes to mind.

Notes

1. Walls, Gary B. "Toward a critical global psychoanalysis." *Psychoanalytic Dialogues* 14.5 (2004): 605–634.
2. Shohat, Ella. "Imaging terra incognita: The disciplinary gaze of empire." *Public Culture* 3.2 (1991): 41–70.
3. Samuels, Robert, and Robert Samuels. "Global solidarity and global government: The universal subject of psychoanalysis and democracy." *Psychoanalyzing the Left and Right after Donald Trump: Conservatism, Liberalism, and Neoliberal Populisms* (2016): 77–101.
4. Žižek, Slavoj. "Looking awry." *October* 50 (1989): 31–55.
5. Peters, Michael A. "The enlightenment and its critics1." *Educational Philosophy and Theory* 51.9 (2019): 886–894.
6. Samuels, Robert, and Robert Samuels. "Beyond Hillary Clinton: Obsessional Narcissism and the Failure of the Liberal Class." *Psychoanalyzing the Left and Right after Donald Trump: Conservatism, Liberalism, and Neoliberal Populisms*(2016): 31–59.
7. Allen, Amy. *The end of progress: Decolonizing the normative foundations of critical theory.* Vol. 36. Columbia University Press, 2016.
8. Rieff, Philip. *Freud: The mind of the moralist.* University of Chicago Press, 1979.
9. Samuels, Robert. "Misunderstanding Psychoanalysis from the Left." *(Mis)Understanding Freud with Lacan, Zizek, and Neuroscience.* Cham: Springer International Publishing, 2022. 159–184.
10. Jameson, Fredric. "Imaginary and symbolic in Lacan: Marxism, psychoanalytic criticism, and the problem of the subject." *Yale French Studies* 55/56 (1977): 338–395.
11. Žižek, Slavoj. "A leftist plea for" Eurocentrism"." *Critical Inquiry*24.4 (1998): 988–1009.
12. Kapoor, Ilan. "Žižek, antagonism and politics now: three recent controversies." *International Journal of Žižek Studies* 12.1 (2018).

13. Kymlicka, Will. "Liberal individualism and liberal neutrality." *Ethics* 99.4 (1989): 883–905.
14. Samuels, Robert, and Robert Samuels. "Pathos, Hysteria, and the Left." *Zizek and the Rhetorical Unconscious: Global Politics, Philosophy, and Subjectivity* (2020): 33–47.
15. Cole, Alyson Manda. *The cult of true victimhood: From the war on welfare to the war on terror.* Stanford University Press, 2007.
16. Rancière, Jacques. "Politics, identification, and subjectivization." *The identity in question.* Routledge, 2014. 63–70.
17. Bouris, Erica. *Complex political victims.* Kumarian Press, 2007.
18. Freud, Sigmund. "The ego and the id (1923)." *TACD Journal*17.1 (1989): 5–22.
19. Freud, Sigmund. *Totem and taboo.* Phoemixx Classics Ebooks, 2021.
20. Henrich, Joseph. *The WEIRDest people in the world: How the West became psychologically peculiar and particularly prosperous.* Penguin UK, 2020.
21. Modell, Arnold H. "The ego and the id: Fifty years later." *The International Journal of Psycho-Analysis* 56 (1975): 57.
22. Hanly, Charles. "Ego ideal and ideal ego." *The International Journal of Psycho-Analysis* 65 (1984): 253.
23. Freud, Sigmund. *Civilization and its discontents.* Broadview Press, 2015.
24. Samuels, Robert. *Psychoanalyzing the politics of the new brain sciences.* Springer, 2017.
25. Khader, Jamil. "Žižek's "Frankenstein": Modernity, Anti-Enlightenment Critique and Debates on the Left." *Enrahonar. An international journal of theoretical and practical reason*(2022): 1–23.
26. Hofstadter, Richard. *Social darwinism in American thought.* Vol. 16. Beacon Press, 1992.
27. Kollai, István. "The many meanings of neo-feudalism Analysis of academic and public discourse alluding premodern social structures." *Köz-gazdaság-Review of Economic Theory and Policy* 15.1 (2020).
28. Ridley, Matt. "e Rational Optimist [Kindle edition] HarperCollins." (2010).
29. Samuels, Robert, and Robert Samuels. "Logos, global justice, and the reality principle." *Zizek and the Rhetorical Unconscious: Global Politics, Philosophy, and Subjectivity*(2020): 65–86.
30. Botticelli, Steven. "Globalization, psychoanalysis, and the provision of care: Roundtable on global woman." *Studies in Gender and Sexuality* 7.1 (2006): 71–80.
31. Poeldinger, W. J. "The psychopathology and psychodynamics of self-destruction." *Crisis: The Journal of Crisis Intervention and Suicide Prevention* (1989).
32. Freud, Sigmund. "Repression." *The Psychoanalytic Review (1913–1957)* 9 (1922): 444.

33. Samuels, Robert, and Robert Samuels. "Pathos, Hysteria, and the Left." *Zizek and the Rhetorical Unconscious: Global Politics, Philosophy, and Subjectivity* (2020): 33–47.
34. Gopal, Abhijit, Robert Willis, and Yasmin Gopal. "From the colonial enterprise to enterprise systems: Parallels between colonization and globalization." *Postcolonial Theory and Organizational Analysis: A Critical Engagement: A Critical Engagement* (2003): 233–254.
35. Henrich, Joseph. *The WEIRDest people in the world: How the West became psychologically peculiar and particularly prosperous*. Penguin UK, 2020.
36. Rossinow, Douglas Charles. *The politics of authenticity: Liberalism, Christianity, and the New Left in America*. Columbia University Press, 1998.
37. Strauß, Harald. "Comparatively Rich and Reactionary: Germany Between "Welcome Culture" and Re-established Racism." *Critical Sociology* 43.1 (2017): 3–10.
38. Kateb, George. "Democratic individualism and its critics." *Annual Review of Political Science* 6.1 (2003): 275–305
39. Kateb, George. *The inner ocean: Individualism and democratic culture*. Cornell University Press, 1992.
40. Svensson, Frances. "Liberal democracy and group rights: the legacy of individualism and its impact on American Indian tribes." *Political Studies* 27.3 (1979): 421–439.
41. Hebert, L. Joseph. *More than kings and less than men: Tocqueville on the promise and perils of democratic individualism*. Lexington Books, 2010.
42. Samuels, Robert, and Robert Samuels. "Logos, global justice, and the reality principle." *Zizek and the Rhetorical Unconscious: Global Politics, Philosophy, and Subjectivity*(2020): 65–86.
43. McCamant, John F. "A critique of present measures of "human rights development" and an alternative." *Global human rights: Public policies, comparative measures, and NGO strategies*. Routledge, 2019. 123–146.
44. Chambers, Stefanie. "Minority empowerment and environmental justice." *Urban affairs review* 43.1 (2007): 28–54.
45. Schachter, Joseph. "Abstinence and neutrality: Development and diverse views." *The International Journal of Psycho-Analysis* 75.4 (1994): 709.
46. Belkin, Max, and Cleonie White, eds. *Intersectionality and relational psychoanalysis: New perspectives on race, gender, and sexuality*. Routledge, 2020.
47. Mitrano, Mena. ""Cogito and the Unconscious", ed. Slavoj Zizek." *College Literature* 27.2 (2000): 201.
48. Moggach, Douglas. "German Idealism and Modernity, or Thinking Freedom." *University of Ottawa. Typescript. Originally published in Portuguese translation, in Douglas Moggach, Hegelianismo, Republicanismo, e Modernidade* (2010).

49. Samuels, Robert. *(Mis) Understanding Freud with Lacan, Zizek, and Neuroscience.* Springer Nature, 2022.
50. Marx, Karl, and Friedrich Engels. *The communist manifesto.* Penguin, 2002.
51. Epstein, Stephan R. "Rodney Hilton, Marxism and the transition from feudalism to capitalism." *Past and Present* 195.suppl_2 (2007): 248–269.
52. Robinson, William I. "Social theory and globalization: The rise of a transnational state." *Theory and society* 30.2 (2001): 157–200.
53. Cousins, Ben. "Capitalism obscured: the limits of law and rights-based approaches to poverty reduction and development." *The Journal of Peasant Studies* 36.4 (2009): 893–908.
54. Pulido, Laura. "Geographies of race and ethnicity II: Environmental racism, racial capitalism and state-sanctioned violence." *Progress in human geography* 41.4 (2017): 524–533.
55. Resnick, Stephen A., and Richard D. Wolff. "Marxist epistemology: The critique of economic determinism." *Social Text* 6 (1982): 31–72.
56. Feher, Ferenc, and Agnes Heller. "Class, democracy, modernity." *Theory and society* 12.2 (1983): 211–244.
57. Schachter, Joseph. "Free association: From Freud to current use—the effects of training analysis on the use of free association." *Psychoanalytic Inquiry* 38.6 (2018): 457–467.
58. Samuels, Robert, and Robert Samuels. "Drugging Discontent: Psychoanalysis, Drives, and the Governmental University Medical Pharmaceutical Complex (GUMP)." *Psychoanalyzing the Politics of the New Brain Sciences* (2017): 115–136.
59. Zizek, Slavoj. Less Than Nothing (p. 727). Verso Books. Kindle Edition.
60. Butler, Judith, et al. *Contingency, hegemony, universality: Contemporary dialogues on the left.* Verso, 2000.
61. Žižek, Slavoj. *The fragile absolute: Or, why is the Christian legacy worth fighting for?.* Verso Books, 2009.
62. Zizek, Slavoj. *Less than nothing: Hegel and the shadow of dialectical materialism.* Verso Books, 2012.

CHAPTER 4

Psychoanalyzing the Right's Rejection of Globalization

Abstract The first thing to understand about the Right-wing rejection of globalization is that it is fundamentally a negative defense mechanism. In other terms, it is not centered on a clear set of political objectivities and policies; rather, it seeks to discredit what it sees at the imposition of a new global social order controlled by Left-wing elites. Although there is clearly a focus in many of these discourses on defending the power and identity of straight white Christian males, these communities are organized around hate, insensitivity, and denial. Moreover, they often function by confusing liberals with centrists and Leftists so that a clear enemy can be defined in a strict binary opposition. They also tend to borrow several of the political and psychological tactics of the Left, and in many ways, they can be read as a dispersed and disorganized counter-revolutionary movement.

Keywords Right-wing • Counter-revolution • Left-wing • Glenn Beck • Conspiracy theories • Borderline personality disorder • Davos • Splitting • Projective identification • The Great Reset

The first thing to understand about the Right-wing rejection of globalization is that it is fundamentally a negative defense mechanism.[1] In other terms, it is not centered on a clear set of political objectivities and policies; rather, it seeks to discredit what it sees at the imposition of a new global social order controlled by Left-wing elites.[2] Although there is clearly a focus in many of these discourses on defending the power and identity of straight white Christian males, these communities are organized around hate, insensitivity, and denial.[3] Moreover, they often function by confusing liberals with centrists and Leftists so that a clear enemy can be defined in a strict binary opposition.[4] They also tend to borrow several of the political and psychological tactics of the Left, and in many ways, they can be read as a dispersed and disorganized counter-revolutionary movement.[5]

From a psychoanalytic perspective, a common driving force of the Right is the refusal of the individual to give up aggressive impulses and the pursuit of the pleasure principle.[6] This defense of individual desire is centered on a fundamental fantasy of total freedom and enjoyment--similar to Freud's theories of the primal horde and the Oedipus Complex.[7] As a mostly masculine social and political reactionary movement, the underlying psychopathology points to a borderline personality disorder structured by low impulse control, splitting, projection, denial, and a hidden fear of abandonment.[8] In other words, Right-wing ideology is not only structured by the defense mechanisms of a borderline personality disorder, but it also attracts people who suffer from this mode of psychopathology.

Like most ideologies and paranoid conspiracy theories, there is often a kernel of truth behind this perspective.[9] In terms of globalization, there has been a loss of employment in developed nations, and many of the people who have lost their jobs and social status do come from the white working class.[10] We have also witnessed a political abandonment by centrist politicians who have responded to de-industrialization by shifting their focus to the upper-middle class professionals.[11] Meanwhile, much of the increase in wealth and income in Western nations has gone to highly educated elites.[12] Thus, even though the global average of per capita income and wealth has increased, these increases have been unevenly shared.[13]

We can therefore admit that there are real reasons for many white working-class males to feel like they have been abandoned by the educated global elites; however, what we need to explain is why this group of resentful citizens have turned to Right-wing ideology to explain their current state.[14] On a basic level, the major reason for the political coalition between low-wage workers and wealthy individuals and corporations is that the Right has used a set of unconscious rhetorical strategies allowing for the ideological combination of opposites.[15] These mainly irrational, symbolic techniques are victim identification, disavowal, over-generalization, denial, splitting, and projection. In other words, the unconscious processes shaping this ideology matches the unconscious psychopathology of the supporters.[16]

Left behind

Since there are so many different aspects to the Right-wing rejection of globalization, it is hard to come up with a common driving force unless we focus on the underlying psychopathology shaping this ideology. In this case, we find in the definition of borderline personality, the key components that structure much of the discourse on the Right.[17] These include poor impulse control, emotional splitting, denial, transient paranoia, and avoidance of abandonment.[18] In fact, the final criteria points to the real underlying cause of much of this reactionary ideology. For it is true that white-working class workers in the West were often left behind by the processes of de-industrialization, outsourcing, automation, and de-unionization caused by the globalization of capitalism and the shift of centrist liberal parties towards upper-middle class elites. Since most of the gains made by workers have been produced in developing countries, the reduction in poverty in one part of the world has resulted in a decrease in economic prosperity in another part.[19]

Instead of understanding this complex and uneven effect of globalization, a form of psychological splitting is applied so that the world is divided into winners and losers on the one hand and victims and perpetrators on the other hand.[20] Moreover, the way that the fear of being abandoned is overcome is by the pursuit of escapist pleasure on the level of the drives, which leads to an increased level of addiction and aggressive impulses.[21] In the borderline battle between the id and the super-ego, the social forces calling for the limitation and renunciation of the drives are externalized and rejected. This process of externalization is coupled with a paranoid use of the primary processes in the form of conspiracy theories.[22]

We thus need psychoanalysis to understand this major resistance to global governance since the Right has proven to be one of the most effective counters to the need for global solutions to global problems. It is also vital to stress that underlining this borderline politics is the drive for unregulated capital accumulation as evidenced by the wealthy corporations and individuals who do not want to pay taxes or have their businesses regulated.[23] In fact, underlying the coalition between the white working class and the super-rich are two fundamental fantasies. One fantasy is based on the desire for unlimited freedom and enjoyment, while the other is based on the notion that one cannot be guilty or ashamed because one is an innocent victim.[24]

The different interests of the Right are also unified by a shared hatred of the what they see as the progressive, socialist, totalitarian Left.[25] However, I am arguing that this bonding over a shared enemy is evident in all political ideologies, and so what makes the ideology of the Right special is the particular combination of social groups supported by an underlying borderline psychopathology.

To help articulate the psychopathology of the Right-wing response to globalization, I will offer a close reading of Glenn Beck's *The Great Reset: Joe Biden and the Rise of Twenty-First-Century Fascism*.[26] Already in the title of the book, one can see how all complexity and nuance is lost by claiming that the moderate Joe Biden is a fascist. Through the use of the irrational symbolic primary processes of hyperbole and over-generalization, Right-wing ideology constructs a paranoid worldview perspective.[27] Moreover, in order to establish a clear distinction between the idealized self and the debased other, a strict binary logic has to be applied, and the way that this opposition is created is by negating differences and drawing metaphorical comparisons that are later taken to be true.[28] Importantly, a central part of this psychopathology is projective identification as a main defense mechanism of borderline personality disorders.[29]

Political Projective Identification

As Otto Kernberg has argued, the primitive unconscious process of splitting is often coupled with a form of projection where one first denies some internal impulse or thought and then experiences that internal experience in others.[30] The next stage is that one attacks the other for what one has projected onto them. Within this mirroring structure, one often finds that the people who have an aggressive drive, attack others for being aggressive.[31] Thus, in the terms of the Right-wing criticism of globalization, the Left is attacked for having fascistic tendencies when it is actually the Right that is more aligned with this ideology.[32]

In terms of political belief systems, it is vital to understand that the contemporary Right has to engage in coded, unconscious processes because their fundamental project is based on a lie.[33] The leaders of this movement cannot say directly that their main goal is to allow for the super-wealthy to make more money, pay lower taxes, and face fewer governmental regulations. Instead, they have to produce a culture war where the white working class is being victimized by the global elites who want to force them to submit to a totalitarian form of socialism.[34] Coupled with this shared conspiracy theory, we find the Right's focus on the hypocrisy of the global elite, and much of this part of their discourse relates to true problems. For instance, when Beck highlights how many of the global elites participating in the World Economic Forum at Davos act in a hypocritical way, he is correct to some degree: "Why are people who claim that climate change is an existential threat to human life building mansions on islands and beaches, despite alleged fears of rising sea levels, and flying around the world in private jets that spew carbon dioxide into the atmosphere?" (12–13). In fact, one of the things that infuriates non-elites is when they see the super-wealthy telling them that they should not do the very things that they do themselves, like using carbon-emitting airplanes.[35] As we shall see in the next chapter, centrist liberals do often act in hypocritical ways, but what Beck leaves out of his own criticism is the fact that many of the people supporting Right-wing ideology are also hypocritical elites.[36]

Through the use of splitting and projective identification, Beck and other Right-wingers often mimic many of the same criticisms that we find on the Left. For instance, in order to appeal to the working class, Beck hides his own elite status and attacks the super-wealthy for destroying the lives of the lower classes:

> The economy, once driven by the wants and needs of the individual consumer, is now guided by an agenda crafted by a cabal of international elites. Despite having been marketed as a solution to all of society's ills, the Great Reset agenda has left everyday Americans worse off than ever before and increasingly dependent on the government and wealthy global corporations that serve as the foundation of this brave and terrifying new world. (16)

At first glance, Beck's critique looks like a Marxist criticism of global capitalism, but it is important to remember that Beck himself has made his career by being supported by a global media corporation.[37] Beck, then, is a global elite, who denies his elite status, and then he projects this elitism onto others, which he in turn, attacks. Furthermore, by claiming that there is a secret cabal, he makes his own analysis into a conspiracy theory.

One of the interesting things about conspiracy theories is that they are often based on detecting a secret that is revealed by a set of signs.[38] Like the return of the repressed, the secret society cannot stop leaving hints about their hidden agenda, and it is the community of interpreters who either are in on the conspiracy or are the victims of its dark intentions.[39] These not-so hidden conspiracies reflect on the way that our minds automatically confuse correlation with causation in a paranoid manner.[40] For example, if someone sees two events happen at the same time, they often believe that one event causes the other. For Freud, at the heart of the primary processes, we find this confusion between mental association and intention, and so from a psychoanalytic perspective, the question is not why are there conspiracy theories; rather, the question is what allows us to escape our automatic compulsion to see connections and project intentions?[41]

One of the main goals of the reality principle and the psychoanalytic process is to learn how to distinguish correlation from causation, and this requires differentiating our memories from our perceptions.[42] Since, as Freud insists, memories work through association and substitution, they are prone to paranoid thinking and the projection of internal thoughts onto the external world.[43] The only way to overcome this tendency of projective paranoia is through a method of critical introspection and radical self-honesty, but this is often hard to do because we do not have complete control over our own minds.

In terms of shared conspiracy theories, a combination of hypnotic suggestion and empathic identification motivates people to unknowingly internalize the same paranoid fantasies.[44] This process is enhanced through the use of mass media and the Web since it is easy for people to find information that feeds into their particular interests and pathologies. As a mode of victim identification, many of these conspiracies share the common narrative of an innocent group of people being exploited by a secret cabal of evil perpetrators.[45]

Matching the victim fantasy in Right-wing discourse, we also find a fantasy of total freedom and enjoyment, which is seen as being under attack. For instance, in the following passage, Beck combines both fundamental fantasies together: "The America we remember, the America of carefree summers, Saturday night trips to movie theaters, warm family holiday gatherings, and mom-and-pop restaurants, has been replaced with a culture driven by suspicion, rampant fear, and ideological and political tribalism and dominated by massive, multinational corporations" (21). As a form of borderline splitting, an idealized past of freedom and pleasure is compared to the debased present, which suffers from the domination of unleashed multinational corporations causing a culture of fear and suspicion. Of course, Beck himself is spreading fear and suspicion at the very moment he accuses others of doing the same thing. As a clear case of projective identification, the Right wants people to blame the Left for everything that Right itself is fomenting.[46]

Similar to the use of hyperbole on the Left, the Right tends to stoke fears and resentments by over-generalizing and exaggerating real problems.[47] Moreover, psychoanalysis tells us that this use of primary processes is mainly unconscious, which means that the people who are engaging in this form of rhetorical manipulation are not directly aware of what they are doing. As a psychopathology, the defense mechanisms of the Right are mostly unintentional, irrational, and indirect, and this is one reason why they are so effective, and it is also one reason why they also appear to be conspiracy theories.

The Great Reset Conspiracy

In many ways, Beck's book is a collection of conspiracy theories, but there is an over-arching theory that brings all of the other theories together, and this concerns the idea of the "Great Reset." Originally, this term was derived from a speech made by Klaus Schwab, the head of the World Economic Forum.[48] For Schwab, the reset involves making global capitalism more socially and environmentally friendly. Although, it is easy to mock this idea since many of the people who promote it are leaders of carbon-producing, inequality-generating multinational corporations and governments, there is no secret plan to impose a global form of fascist socialism as Beck and others on the Right claim.[49] Yet, Beck wants to insist that this global conspiracy is real, and it is spreading to all aspects of our lives: "The Great Reset is a proposal that is breathtaking in its scope. Its backers support altering nearly every part of society, from the cars we drive to the food we eat to the news reports we watch on television. Its core foundation was shaped almost entirely by a small, extremely wealthy and well-connected group of people, one that includes highly influential business leaders, environmentalists, government officials, and bankers" (22). Although, part of this analysis is true—there really was a meeting of wealthy elites talking about how to change the global economy--, it is absurd to claim that they want to change every part of our lives.

One of the major problems with these Right-wing conspiracies is that not only do they help destructive leaders gain power, but they also distort what is really happening with globalization: "The goal of the Great Reset is both shocking and wildly ambitious: to transform the global economy, eliminate free markets, impose a new, more easily controllable and malleable economic system, and change the way people think about private property and corporations. The reset part of the Great Reset is an allusion to "pushing the reset button" on the global economy—and boy, do they want to push that sucker hard" (22). Beck's Right-wing extremism is on full display in this claim that the leaders of global capital want to eliminate free markets and private property.[50] One reason why he may be making such an exaggerated claim is that like so many other promoters of Right-wing ideology, his main goal is to attract an audience and cash in on their rage and resentment.[51] In fact, Beck's discourse is shaped by the contemporary combination of journalism, entertainment, and business, and while he does not discuss his own true motivations, he is quick to attack others for their hypocrisy and secret plots.[52]

One of the reoccurring aspects of contemporary Right-wing conspiracy theories is the idea that every real crisis is actually a fake emergency produced by elites and liberals who seek to take advantage of dire situations: "In early June 2020, the World Economic Forum (WEF), a large non-profit based in Switzerland, held a virtual meeting featuring many of the most powerful people on the face of the planet. The purpose of the meeting was to launch a new campaign for a Great Reset of the global economy, using the COVID-19 pandemic and climate change as justifications for their proposed reforms to society" (22–23). Once again, the problem with this extreme claim is that is undermines the real risks facing the world in order to demonize a political opponent and trigger the anger of the intended audience.[53]

In an act of projective identification, Beck attacks his opponents for doing exactly what he is doing himself, which is pretending to care about the working class as he helps to support the agenda of wealthy elites: "The Davos crowd often gets a bad rap for hosting lavish parties after spending long days lamenting about the plight of the common man, but I think we should give them a break. After all, scheming about the best ways to lord over the entire world in between ski trips is hard work" (23). This focus on lavish parties represents the Right's tendency to be resentful of anyone else's enjoyment since from their constant-sum perspective, someone else's pleasure means that there is less pleasure for themselves.[54] Similar to Ronald Reagan's claim that the poor are "welfare queens," the Right is always on the lookout to condemn other people's possible enjoyment.[55]

This attack on the enjoyment of the other is clearest in the rejection of social programs that redistribute resources from the wealthy to the impoverished: "One of the ways in which Great Reset supporters like Burrow want to design a better world is by engaging in massive wealth redistribution schemes, ones that would promote economic "equality," not only among citizens within individual nations but also between countries" (24). This fear of equality and the redistribution of wealth is in part driven by the desire of the super-rich to avoid paying taxes: On its most fundamental level, the Right-wing counter-revolution is a tax revolt from above as the people with the most resources refuse to share with others.[56]

All of the attacks on redistribution, socialism, and equality have at their roots, the borderline subject's desire to pursue selfish pleasure at all costs.[57] Like two-year old children who are bent on expressing their individualism by saying no to any parental regulation, the Right feeds a mentality of greedy, anti-social desire.[58] As an embodiment of the Oedipus Complex, the desire for unlimited enjoyment is coupled with a hatred for anyone who gets in the way. Therefore, we should rethink Freud's original Oedipus Complex as more than the male child's desire for the mother and hatred of the intervening father; instead, it is vital to see how anti-social drives are reliant on a rejection of social regulation and the sharing of resources.[59]

For Beck, the conflict between the selfish greed of the free individual and the hated restrictions of the social other are represented by the battle between Right-wing libertarians, like Trump, and their liberal, globalist opposition: "President Biden's role in this movement cannot be understated. The moment he became president, the U.S. government's unofficial platform immediately and dramatically shifted from President Trump's "America First" agenda to the globalist Great Reset" (26). It is of course absurd to call Biden a totalitarian socialist globalist, but if you listen to Fox News or many other Right-wing news outlets, there is often no distinction made between centrists, liberals, Leftists, socialists, communists, and fascists.[60] Anyone who resists the agenda of the Right is labeled an enemy of the people and a part of the global conspiracy to end private property and individual freedom.

Perhaps the greatest irony of the Great Reset conspiracy theory is the notion that the people who are leading us towards a totalitarian mode of socialism are the largest banks, corporations, and financial institutions: "For now, it is vital that you keep in mind that the plan for a Great Reset is not some far-off, left-wing European fantasy that has little or nothing to do with America. Many of the most important figures tied to the Great Reset are, in fact, American. And most of the large corporations, banks, and financial institutions that have backed the plan are also from the United States or have significant financial ties to the country" (26). Beck wants his audience to know that in this upside-down world, it is the wealthy capitalists who are against capitalism, and the liberal democracies that are pursuing fascism. As a mode of ideological gaslighting, people's perceptions of reality are undermined as absurd distortions of reality are presented.[61] In fact, what we find with borderline personalities is that they often attack others when they feel that their own aggression and enjoyment is being exposed. In this case, it is not Beck and his cronies who are seeking to pursue money and power at all costs: The Real perpetrators are the people trying to address climate change, pandemics, war, and poverty.[62]

Conspiracies about Conspiracies

One of the problems in trying to critique this Right-wing, anti-globalization discourse is that it is hard not to sound like a conspiracy theorist when one is exposing the irrationality of conspiracy theories. This issue is in part due to the fact that the Right tends to use projective identification to escape any sense of guilt, shame, or responsibility.[63] For example, in the following claim, Beck seeks to project his own paranoia onto the people he is attacking: "the Great Reset is indeed a wild, crazy, completely out-there conspiracy, it is a very real one—and it has the potential to dramatically alter our world forever" (27). By claiming that the global elites are participating in a real conspiracy, he attempts to render his own conspiracy theory valid and rational. Moreover, just as the Right has learned to keep its appeal to racism coded and indirect, Beck posits that the Left is hiding their true fascist agenda behind capitalist rhetoric[64]:

> The Great Reset's biggest advocates never use the words fascism or authoritarianism to describe the Reset or their agenda. They have worked very hard to integrate capitalistic language like markets and investments into their plans, and many have even tried to frame the Great Reset's provisions as creating a new kind of capitalism—so-called stakeholder capitalism—while simultaneously talking about ending many of the world's markets. (27)

As part of the supposed hypocrisy of the global liberal-Left, Beck reveals the way multinational corporations and their leaders tend to use socially progressive rhetoric to hide their true intentions.[65] On one level, Beck is correct here, but his own analysis is undermined when he goes to the extreme and claims that global capitalists are against capitalism.

The Hypnotic Right

As Zizek often jokes, a man who accuses his wife of cheating on him may still be paranoid even if the wife is really having an affair.[66] The real issue is why does the man want to believe in the infidelity of his wife. Freud found that the paranoid man is often projecting his own illicit desires onto others so that he can condemn his own impulses from a disavowed distance.[67] In the Right's case, the use of conspiracy theories is denied and projected onto others at the very moment conspiracies are being fabricated. For instance, Beck tells his readers that they need to learn how to connect the dots to see how all of the different conspiracies he is articulating relate to each other.

> On the surface, many of these ideas can seem agonizingly tedious and even downright boring, especially when you look at them on their own. But once you realize that each of these ideas is a puzzle piece that connects to form a much larger, more transformative and radical scheme, it is easy to see why powerful people around the world are pushing so hard to promote the Great Reset, and why I'm working so hard to fight against it. (28)

Since Beck claims that he knows the secret truth of a global conspiracy, he argues that his paranoid interpretation actually represents reality. While it is not always clear whether these Right-wing charlatans know what they are doing, it does not really matter because their audience tends to think in a paranoid way.[68] Like the people attending a professional wrestling show, once the performance begins, disbelief is suspended, and people get immersed in the fake reality they are perceiving.[69] In fact, most of our media consumption relies on this type of hypnotic effect and regression, and so it should not be surprising if the growing dominance of the new Right has been achieved at the same times as the culture industry has extended its reach into our lives.[70]

From a psychoanalytic perspective, the combination of hypnosis and addiction helps to explain how people can becomes so susceptible to the suggestions they hear in the media.[71] Since hypnosis is based on suspending reality testing by regressing to the relation between the helpless subject and the all-powerful Other, media immersion makes people prone to being influenced by conspiracy theories.[72] Furthermore, the compulsive watching of the news represents a mode of media addiction, which serves to provide pleasure by allowing for an escape from reality.[73] When you then combine addictive viewing with hypnotic suggestion and conspiracy theories, you end up with a large group of people who are prone to believe any propaganda that is placed before them.[74]

Fascism and the Right

In many ways, it is the Right that borrows techniques and arguments from fascism in order to motivate white working-class males to internalize a message that they are the true victims, and the people trying to improve the world are the true victimizers.[75] Of course, Beck turns this fascistic propaganda on its head by arguing that the real fascists are liberal centrists:

> Unlike many other troubling plans promoted in the past by elites in government and business, the Great Reset is not dangerous because it could lead to soft authoritarianism or a form of fascism at some distant moment in the future. It is dangerous because it is soft authoritarianism and it is a new kind of fascism. It has merely been carefully rebranded as a variation of capitalism, an "inclusive capitalism," in order to fool well-meaning people—on the political left and right—who otherwise would never want the United States to adopt Great Reset ideas.

In this moment of projective identification, Beck accuses liberal democracies of being fascistic as he himself employs the techniques of fascism.[76]

Although fascists like Hitler did have to rely on direct violence in order to impose their authoritarian desires, they also manipulated the masses through propaganda and conspiracy theories.[77] Beck believes that the current quest of the liberal-Left to impose their totalitarian ideology on the world may not require the same level of violence used by past fascistic states, but he thinks that the effect will be the same:

> The Great Reset will not necessarily require the mass imprisonment of dissenters, nationwide confiscation of businesses, or a bloody revolution. It can achieve authoritarian goals without jackbooted storm troopers or gulags, and it includes just enough elements of cronyism and payouts to global elites to make the system palatable to the world's wealthiest and most well-connected people. It is a kind of authoritarian, international, socialistic

fascism, yes, but it's not Marx's socialism or the fascistic models embraced by Benito Mussolini. It is authoritarianism for our brand-new technology-rich, corrupt era. It is twenty-first century fascism. (29)

On one level, this projection of fascism onto the global capitalists helps to deny the real fascistic tendencies on the Right, but on another level, it also distorts the power of the owners of new high-tech multinational corporations. The strange misrepresentation of global capitalism mainly serves the purpose of feeding the Right-wing audience's fantasies of victimhood.

In displacing the real causes for concern, the Right not only scapegoats particular groups, but it also fails to see that we really do need global solutions to climate change, pandemics, poverty, and war.[78] Instead of endorsing global solutions to global problems, Beck argues that the needed responses are actually the problem and not the solution:

> Instead the Great Reset program is designed to move the world toward collectivism and soft authoritarianism through a combination of new monetary policies, tax regimes designed to punish "undesirable" industries, huge new "green" infrastructure plans, and sweeping social programs that seek to make the vast majority of people, including many in the middle class, dependent on collective institutions and government programs. And rather than confiscate businesses on behalf of the collective or mandate that they become socialist enterprises, the Great Reset's twenty-first century fascist policies would use the power of money printing to coerce and control the world's most influential and powerful businesses, allowing governments to manipulate society and economic activity in unprecedented ways. (30)

As part of the fifty-year libertarian attack on government, the Right undermines any organized public response to pressing social issues because of the fear of increased taxes and enhanced government regulations.[79] However, the only way we can fight climate change, pandemics, poverty, and war is if different countries come together to support coordinated responses. For example, one of the reasons why many individual nations do not have enough funds to support their own social welfare programs is that it is hard to tax multinational corporations and global elites.[80] The only real solution is to have a global tax regime, which will require some form of global enforcement.[81] Likewise, the only way to protect workers against wage theft and abuse is to have global standards since labor has been globalized.[82] Yet, this need for global cooperation should not be confused with some type of global totalitarian government.[83]

Like the European Union and the United States, it is possible to maintain separate nation-states or individual state governments and still have a federal, global, or regional organization.[84] In fact, I will argue in the next chapter that we need to expand the power and reach of institutions like the United Nations in order to universalize human rights, worker protections, and the response to climate change. The trick is to enhance global solidarity while still allowing for democratic participation and transparency, but Right-wing conspiracy theories make this needed change difficult because any effort at global coordination is seen as being a mode of totalitarian subjection:

> The Great Reset is not socialism, even though it does include some socialistic government programs. It isn't free market economics, because elites, governments, and central banks control and even micromanage economic decision making. The Great Reset is full of corporatism, but it is so much more than big bailouts and sweetheart deals between businesses and corrupt politicians. Technology is a huge part of the Reset, but calling it a technocracy fails to capture the full weight of the Reset's transformation of economic and societal activity. The Great Reset is highly fascistic but not violent or nationalistic, like many of the fascist systems of Europe in the twentieth century. (30–31)

Since traditionally, fascism involves extreme nationalism, it is hard to understand what kind of political model Beck is actually representing.[85] The one moment when he does appear to directly define what type of world he is fighting against, he ends up with a strange collage of different political ideologies: "The most accurate name for the Reset is probably something like "modern corporate cronyist techno socialistic international fascism" (31). This bizarre mélange of opposing political structures touches on real threats to liberal democracy and global progress, but the use of hyperbole and a lack of distinctions makes the threat both overwhelming and amorphous.

It turns out that the main model for Beck's enemy is China, which is seen as combining all of the different threatening aspects with which the Right is often concerned: "you will probably notice throughout this book the Great Reset's parallels to the Chinese "capitalist" economic model, which has for decades attempted to blend corruption, technology, despotism, and corporatism together into a soft-authoritarian smoothie that tastes a lot like the delectable poison being peddled under the Great Reset brand today" (31). On some level, Beck's description of China has elements of truth because of its combination of capitalism, authoritarianism, and science.[86] As a combination between premodern hierarchy and modern science, technology and capitalism, China does represent a perplexing political ideology.[87] While it is clearly not a dictatorship of the proletariat, it also does not allow for a totally free market.[88]

In fact, Beck is correct to point out that some elites from the developed West tend to admire China's authoritarian government even if it leads to human rights abuses and a lack of democratic law: "For many years, elites in the West have watched with deep admiration the Chinese government achieve an economic transformation at breakneck speed. And on more than several hundred occasions, they have openly remarked with amazement about China's ability to get the job done, while also quietly muttering concerns about China's record of abusing human rights" (31). Although parts of this analysis are correct, what makes it a fictional conspiracy theory are the notions that China is trying to impose its type of government on the rest of the world, and the idea that the world's biggest banks and corporations are secretly working with China to attain this goal of a global authoritarian regime: "The Great Reset is, in a very real sense, Western elites' attempt at improving upon the China model, which probably explains why the World Economic Forum—which, remember, is one of the key players in the promotion of the Great Reset—has numerous close ties with important figures in China, including Chinese leaders who have served on WEF's board of trustees" (31). The real fact of the matter is that many of the leaders of the World Economic Forum are very concerned about China's growing influence and the totalitarian aspects of their government.[89] It is therefore absurd to claim that China is the model for the centrist global elites.

As I will argue in the next chapter, the real problem with the centrist elites driving globalization is that they often combine a concern for inequality and poverty with an underlying desire to exploit unequal systems for their own personal advantage. These global elites are not trying to impose an international form of authoritarian capitalism; rather, they seek to make small improvements in the developing world as they keep markets open for wealthy individuals and multinational corporations. However, since critics on the Right are so focused on showing a a secret move towards fascism, they are unable to work against the real problems facing our globalizing world.

Notes

1. Hirschberger, Gilad, and Tsachi Ein-Dor. "Defenders of a lost cause: Terror management and violent resistance to the disengagement plan." *Personality and Social Psychology Bulletin* 32.6 (2006): 761–769.
2. Grumke, Thomas. "Globalized anti-globalists: The ideological basis of the internationalization of right-wing extremism." *Right-Wing Radicalism Today*. Routledge, 2013. 27–35.
3. Swank, Duane, and Hans-Georg Betz. "Globalization, the welfare state and right-wing populism in Western Europe." *Socio-Economic Review* 1.2 (2003): 215–245.
4. Samuels, Robert. *The psychopathology of political ideologies*. Routledge, 2021.
5. Rodrik, Dani. "Why does globalization fuel populism? Economics, culture, and the rise of right-wing populism." *Annual Review of Economics* 13 (2021): 133–170.
6. Samuels, Robert, and Robert Samuels. "Catharsis: The politics of enjoyment." *Zizek and the Rhetorical Unconscious. Global Politics, Philosophy, and Subjectivity* (2020): 7–31.
7. Freud, Sigmund. *Totem and taboo*. Phoemixx Classics Ebooks, 2021.
8. Zanarini, Mary C., Jolie L. Weingeroff, and Frances R. Frankenburg. "Defense mechanisms associated with borderline personality disorder." *Journal of personality disorders* 23.2 (2009): 113–121.
9. Shermer, Michael. *The believing brain: From ghosts and gods to politics and conspiracies---How we construct beliefs and reinforce them as truths*. Macmillan, 2011.
10. Hellier, Joël, and Nathalie Chusseau. "Globalization and the Inequality–unemployment Tradeoff." *Review of International Economics* 18.5 (2010): 1028–1043.
11. Hedges, Chris. *Death of the liberal class*. Vintage Canada, 2011.
12. Dollar, David. "Globalization, inequality, and poverty since 1980." *Washington, DC: World Bank* (2001).
13. Kremer, Michael, and Eric Maskin. "Globalization and inequality." (2006): 388–418.
14. Gidron, Noam, and Peter A. Hall. "The politics of social status: Economic and cultural roots of the populist right." *The British journal of sociology* 68 (2017): S57-S84.
15. Samuels, Robert, and Robert Samuels. "Trump and Sanders on the Couch: Neoliberal Populism on the Left and the Right." *Psychoanalyzing the Left and Right after Donald Trump: Conservatism, Liberalism, and Neoliberal Populisms* (2016): 61–76.
16. Samuels, Robert. *The psychopathology of political ideologies*. Routledge, 2021.
17. Kernberg, Otto F., and Robert Michels. "Borderline personality disorder." *American Journal of Psychiatry* 166.5 (2009): 505–508.

18. Gunderson, John G. "Borderline personality disorder: ontogeny of a diagnosis." *American Journal of Psychiatry* 166.5 (2009): 530–539.
19. Sheppard, Eric. "Trade, globalization and uneven development: Entanglements of geographical political economy." *Progress in Human Geography* 36.1 (2012): 44–71.
20. Fertuck, Eric A., Stephanie Fischer, and Joseph Beeney. "Social cognition and borderline personality disorder: splitting and trust impairment findings." *Psychiatric Clinics* 41.4 (2018): 613–632.
21. Kienast, Thorsten, et al. "Borderline personality disorder and comorbid addiction: epidemiology and treatment." *Deutsches Arzteblatt International* 111.16 (2014): 280–286.
22. Steiner, John. "The border between the paranoid-schizoid and the depressive positions in the borderline patient." *British Journal of Medical Psychology* 52.4 (1979): 385–391.
23. Martin, Isaac William. *The permanent tax revolt: How the property tax transformed American politics*. Stanford University Press, 2008.
24. Samuels, Robert, and Robert Samuels. "Victim politics: Psychoanalyzing the neoliberal conservative counter-revolution." *Psychoanalyzing the Left and Right after Donald Trump: Conservatism, Liberalism, and Neoliberal Populisms* (2016): 7–29.
25. Post, Jerrold M. "Terrorism and right-wing extremism: the changing face of terrorism and political violence in the twenty-first century: the virtual community of hatred." *International journal of group psychotherapy* 65.2 (2015): 242–271.
26. Beck, Glenn; Haskins, Justin Trask. The Great Reset: Joe Biden and the Rise of Twenty-First-Century Fascism (pp. 12–13). Forefront Books. Kindle Edition.
27. Hofitadier, Richard. "Paranoid Style." (1966).
28. Lauriola, Marco, Renato Foschi, and Luca Marchegiani. "Integrating values and cognitive style in a model of right-wing radicalism." *Personality and Individual Differences* 75 (2015): 147–153.
29. Zanarini, Mary C., Jolie L. Weingeroff, and Frances R. Frankenburg. "Defense mechanisms associated with borderline personality disorder." *Journal of personality disorders* 23.2 (2009): 113–121.
30. Kernberg, Otto F. "Projection and projective identification: Developmental and clinical aspects." *Journal of the American Psychoanalytic Association* 35.4 (1987): 795–819.
31. Leichsenring, Falk. "Primitive defense mechanisms in schizophrenics and borderline patients." *The Journal of nervous and mental disease* 187.4 (1999): 229–236.
32. Caramani, Daniele, and Luca Manucci. "National past and populism: the re-elaboration of fascism and its impact on right-wing populism in Western Europe." *West European Politics* 42.6 (2019): 1159–1187.

33. Wodak, Ruth. "The politics of fear: What right-wing populist discourses mean." *The Politics of Fear* (2015): 1–256.
34. Korolczuk, Elżbieta. "The roots of right-wing populism in Central and Eastern Europe: at the nexus of neoliberalism and the global culture wars." URL: https://blogs. Lse. ac. uk/eurocrisispress/2019/11/08/the-roots-of-right-wing-populism-in-central-and-eastern-europe-at-the-nexus-of-neoliberalism-and-the-global-culture-wars/ (дата обращения: 17.11. 2021).
35. Parker, Martin. "Catherine Weaver: Hypocrisy Trap: The World Bank and the Poverty of Reform." (2009): 540–542.
36. Pierson, Paul. "American hybrid: Donald Trump and the strange merger of populism and plutocracy." *The British journal of sociology* 68 (2017): S105-S119.
37. Jutel, Olivier. "American populism, Glenn Beck and affective media production." *International Journal of cultural studies* 21.4 (2018): 375–392.
38. Jutel, Olivier. "American populism, Glenn Beck and affective media production." *International Journal of cultural studies* 21.4 (2018): 375–392.
39. Rothschild, Mike. *The storm is upon us: How QAnon became a movement, cult, and conspiracy theory of everything.* Melville House, 2021.
40. Greenburgh, Anna, and Nichola J. Raihani. "Paranoia and conspiracy thinking." *Current Opinion in Psychology* (2022): 101362.
41. Samuels, Robert, and Robert Samuels. "The unconscious and the primary processes." *Freud for the Twenty-First Century: The Science of Everyday Life* (2019): 27–42.
42. Freud, Sigmund, Marie Ed Bonaparte, Anna Ed Freud, Ernst Ed Kris, Eric Trans Mosbacher, and James Trans Strachey. "Project for a scientific psychology." (1954).
43. Murstein, Bernard I., and Ronald S. Pryer. "The concept of projection: A review." *Psychological Bulletin* 56.5 (1959): 353.
44. Freud, Sigmund. *Group Psychology and the Analysis of the Ego.* Read Books Ltd., 2014.
45. Zizek, S. (1994). Ideology between fiction and fantasy. *Cardozo L. Rev.*, 16, 1511.
46. Moses, Rafael. "Projection, identification, and projective identification: their relation to political process." *Projection, identification, projective identification.* Routledge, 2018. 133–150.
47. Samuels, Robert, and Robert Samuels. "Pathos, Hysteria, and the Left." *Zizek and the Rhetorical Unconscious: Global Politics, Philosophy, and Subjectivity* (2020): 33–47.
48. Schwab, Klaus, and Thierry Malleret. "The great reset." *World economic forum, Geneva.* Vol. 22. 2020.
49. Engesser, Sven, et al. "Populism and social media: How politicians spread a fragmented ideology." *Information, communication & society* 20.8 (2017): 1109–1126.

50. Christensen, Michael, and Ashli Au. "The Great Reset and the Cultural Boundaries of Conspiracy Theory." *International Journal of Communication* 17 (2023): 19.
51. Cosentino, Gabriele. "From Pizzagate to the great replacement: the globalization of conspiracy theories." *Social media and the post-truth world order*. Palgrave Pivot, Cham, 2020. 59–86.
52. Rogers, Karl Alan. *Debunking Glenn Beck: How to save America from media pundits and propagandists*. ABC-CLIO, 2011.
53. Emmens, H. *Conspiracy Theories in a Populist Right-Wing Party*. BS thesis. University of Twente, 2021.
54. Davis, Colin, and Colin Davis. "Conclusion: Tarrying with the Negative." *Ethical Issues in Twentieth-Century French Fiction: Killing the Other* (2000): 189–195.
55. Kohler-Hausmann, Julilly. "Welfare crises, penal solutions, and the origins of the "welfare queen"." *Journal of Urban History* 41.5 (2015): 756–771.
56. Block, Fred. "Read their lips: Taxation and the right-wing agenda." *The New Fiscal Sociology: taxation in comparative and historical perspective* (2009): 68–85.
57. Boyer, L. Bryce. "Working with a borderline patient." *The Psychoanalytic Quarterly* 46.3 (1977): 386–424.
58. Cartwright, Duncan. "'Terrible twos': Developing the capacity to think and feel in the analytic field." *Psycho-analytic Psychotherapy in South Africa* 27.1 (2019): 34–57.
59. Paris, Joel. "The Oedipus complex: A critical re-examination." *Canadian Psychiatric Association Journal* 21.3 (1976): 173–179.
60. Phillips, Whitney. "The house that fox built: Anonymous, spectacle, and cycles of amplification." *Television & New Media* 14.6 (2013): 494–509.
61. Shane, Tommy, Tom Willaert, and Marc Tuters. "The rise of "gaslighting": debates about disinformation on Twitter and 4chan, and the possibility of a "good echo chamber"." *Popular communication* 20.3 (2022): 178–192.
62. Fielitz, Maik, and Holger Marcks. "Digital Fascism." *Challenges for the Open Society in Times of Social Media. UC Berkeley: Center for Right-Wing Studies*. URL: https://escholarship. Org/uc/item/87w5c5gp (Abruf: 15.03. 2020) (2019).
63. Messina, Karyne E. *Resurgence of Global Populism: A Psychoanalytic Study of Projective Identification, Blame-shifting and the Corruption of Democracy*. Taylor & Francis, 2022.
64. Haney-López, Ian. *Dog whistle politics: How coded racial appeals have reinvented racism and wrecked the middle class*. Oxford University Press, 2014.
65. Klein, Naomi. *No logo*. Vintage Canada, 2009.

66. Žižek, Slavoj. *The matrix, or, the two sides of perversion.* Springer Netherlands, 2006.
67. Freud, Sigmund. *The Schreber Case.* Penguin, 2003.
68. Weinberg, Bill. "9/11 at Nine: The Conspiracy Industry and the Lure of Fascism." *Anarchist Developments in Cultural Studies* 1 (2011).
69. Craven, Gerald, and Richard Moseley. "Actors on the canvas stage: The dramatic conventions of professional wrestling." *Journal of popular culture* 6.2 (1972): 327.
70. Samuels, Robert, and Robert Samuels. "The pleasure principle and the death drive." *Freud for the Twenty-First Century: The Science of Everyday Life* (2019): 17–25.
71. Junqueira, Luis Fernando Bernardi. "The power within: Mass media, scientific entertainment, and the introduction of psychical research into China, 1900–1920." *Journal of the History of the Behavioral Sciences* (2022).
72. Dawson, Paul. "Conspiracy Theories and Journalistic Emplotment in the Age of Social Media." *The Routledge Companion to Narrative Theory* (2022).
73. Nakaya, Andrea C. "Internet and social media addiction." *Webology* 12.2 (2015): 1–3.
74. Melley, Timothy. *Empire of conspiracy: The culture of paranoia in postwar America.* Cornell University Press, 2017.
75. Nagle, Angela. *Kill all normies: Online culture wars from 4chan and Tumblr to Trump and the alt-right.* John Hunt Publishing, 2017.
76. Vivian, Bradford. "The incitement: An account of language, power, and fascism." *Rhetoric Society Quarterly* 51.5 (2021): 361–376.
77. O'Shaughnessy, Nicholas. "Selling Hitler: propaganda and the Nazi brand." *Journal of Public Affairs: An International Journal* 9.1 (2009): 55–76.
78. Berlet, Chip. "The violence of right-wing populism." *Peace Review* 7.3–4 (1995): 283–288.
79. Rosen, Elliot A. *The Republican Party in the Age of Roosevelt: Sources of Anti-Government Conservatism in the United States.* University of Virginia Press, 2014.
80. Saxunova, Darina, and Rita Szarkova. "Global efforts of tax authorities and tax evasion challenge." *Journal of Eastern Europe Research in Business and Economics* 2018 (2018): 1–14.
81. Kerzner, David S., and David W. Chodikoff. *International tax evasion in the global information age.* Springer, 2016.
82. Hartman, Laura P., Bill Shaw, and Rodney Stevenson. "Exploring the ethics and economics of global labor standards: A challenge to integrated social contract theory." *Business Ethics Quarterly* 13.2 (2003): 193–220.
83. Bostrom, Nick, and Milan M. Cirkovic, eds. *Global catastrophic risks.* Oxford University Press, 2011.

84. Kohler-Koch, Beate. "The organization of interests and democracy in the European Union." *Debating the democratic legitimacy of the European Union* (2007): 255–271.
85. Gentile, Emilio. *The struggle for modernity: Nationalism, futurism, and fascism*. Greenwood Publishing Group, 2003.
86. Witt, Michael A., and Gordon Redding. "Authoritarian capitalism." *The Oxford handbook of Asian business systems* (2014): 26.
87. McGregor, James. *No ancient wisdom, no followers: The challenges of Chinese authoritarian capitalism*. Easton Studio Press, LLC, 2012.
88. Hofman, Peter S., Jeremy Moon, and Bin Wu. "Corporate social responsibility under authoritarian capitalism: Dynamics and prospects of state-led and society-driven CSR." *Business & Society* 56.5 (2017): 651–671.
89. Storey, Ian, and Herbert Yee, eds. *The China threat: perceptions, myths and reality*. Routledge, 2004.

Against political ideology and ideal economic models, Stiglitz sought to base policy on objective reason and a careful unbiased analysis of imperfect information.[6] Like Freud's attempt to apply rationality to irrational human thoughts and actions, his turn to information economics allowed for a more realistic approach to capitalist markets:

> The standard models that economists had used for generations argued either that markets worked perfectly—some even denied the existence of genuine unemployment—or that the only reason that unemployment existed was that wages were too high, suggesting the obvious remedy: lower wages. Information economics, with its better analyses of labor, capital, and product markets, enabled the construction of macroeconomic models that provided deeper insights into unemployment, models that explained the fluctuations, the recessions and depressions, that had marked capitalism since its beginnings. (xii)

Stiglitz posits here that global economic policy has to be more nuanced, complex, and open since markets often rely on incomplete information and irrational actors.[7]

The main model and theory Stiglitz had to fight against was the libertarian fantasy that left on their own, markets will correct themselves: "The IMF's policies, in part based on the outworn presumption that markets, by themselves, lead to efficient outcomes, failed to allow for desirable government interventions in the market, measures which can guide economic growth and make everyone better off" (xii).[8] Against this free market ideology, Stiglitz clearly believes that governments need to intervene in global markets in order to make them more efficient and fair, and a key for this type of public policy is the use of data to guide decisions:

> My research on information made me particularly attentive to the consequences of the lack of information. I was glad to see the emphasis during the global financial crisis in 1997–98 of the importance of transparency; but saddened by the hypocrisy that the institutions, the IMF and the U.S. Treasury, which emphasized it in East Asia, were among the least transparent that I had encountered in public life. This is why in the discussion of reform I emphasize the necessity for increased transparency, improving the information that citizens have about what these institutions do, allowing those who are affected by the policies to have a greater say in their formulation. (xii)

In contrast to the notion that global elites want to run the world through the implementation of secret strategies, Stiglitz insists that our public institutions must be transparent so that everyone will have the information they need to understand what is happening.[9] Unfortunately, he found that when he worked at these major global institutions, there was a tendency to act in secret, which not only deprives citizens of needed information but also serves to feed conspiracy theories.[10]

The Psychopathology of Centrist Narcissism

In terms of modern science and liberal democracy, the twin engines that should be driving global public policy, it is necessary to be open and flexible; however, Stiglitz believes that this type of unbiased reason is often subverted by standardized models and partisan ideologies:

> When crises hit, the IMF prescribed outmoded, inappropriate, if "standard" solutions, without considering the effects they would have on the people in the countries told to follow these policies. Rarely did I see forecasts about what the policies would do to poverty. Rarely did I see thoughtful discussions and analyses of the consequences of alternative policies. There was a single prescription. Alternative opinions were not sought. Open, frank discussion was discouraged—there was no room for it. Ideology guided policy prescription and countries were expected to follow the IMF guidelines without debate. (xiv)

Stiglitz highlights here a major issue with the ideology and psychology of central elites: Unlike, true modern liberals, the professional upper-middle class tends to replace reason with ideology, and this ideology often promotes the interests of their own group over others.[11] Since these experts want to be seen as being right and good, they have a hard time admitting when their policies fail.[12] They also often pretend to be democratic, while in reality, they rely only on people belonging to their same group and class. This insularity can make global elites insensitive to the real suffering of others as it also undermines the trust people have in a group that refuses to be transparent.

In my analysis of what I have called centrist narcissism, I argue that this ideology and psychopathology is based on need for people to believe that they are good and competent, and the main way that they prove to themselves that they are good is by having others recognize their virtues.[13] This

One of the main issues with centrist narcissists is that they are often highly educated and intelligent, but they lack insight into the lives and desires of people coming from a different class or culture.[21] A possible source for this problem is that so much of academic theory comes from a small group of what Henrich calls WEIRD people (Western, Educated, Industrial, Rich, Democratic).[22] Although this group only makes up a small part of the world's population, they dominate higher education and political institutions. As the product of elite meritocratic institutions, their knowledge and beliefs are mostly produced by the same rarefied global elites.[23] However, instead of seeing this system as a conspiracy, we should realize the truth of Marx's idea that the ruling ideas of a culture are shaped by the ruling class.[24]

As Stiglitz admits, one of the ruling ideas created by the ruling global class is the notion that developing nations should improve their economies by opening up their markets to external investments and global trade:

> Today, few—apart from those with vested interests who benefit from keeping out the goods produced by the poor countries—defend the hypocrisy of pretending to help developing countries by forcing them to open up their markets to the goods of the advanced industrial countries while keeping their own markets protected, policies that make the rich richer and the poor more impoverished—and increasingly angry. (xv)

On one level, this process of liberalization has actually helped some nations enhance their standard of living, but in many cases, the real effect was that internal and external elites made most of the profits, while the masses experienced slight improvements or increased poverty.[25]

Once again, it is this hypocrisy that often angers the anti-globalists on the Left and the Right. In fact, for Stiglitz, the major problem with structural adjustments is that the people imposing them are insular and refuse to correct failed policies:

> What astounded me, however, was that those policies weren't questioned by many of the people in power in the IMF, by those who were making the critical decisions. They were often questioned by people in the developing countries, but many were so afraid they might lose IMF funding, and with it funding from others, that they articulated their doubts most cautiously, if at all, and then only in private. But while no one was happy about the suffering that often accompanied the IMF programs, inside the IMF it was simply assumed that whatever suffering occurred was a necessary part of the

form of virtue signaling often alienates outsiders because it appears to be false and hypocritical, and in many instances, it is.[14] As Freud discovered in his analysis of obsessive-compulsive neurosis, altruistic actions are sometimes driven by a desire to hide hostile impulses.[15] In the case of centrsit politics, we find that the attempts to promote diversity, equity, and inclusion are sometimes driven by an underlying sense of shame and guilt.[16] By pretending to care about the victims of inequality, the meritocratic elite are able to assuage their conscience as they continue to exploit the advantages generated out of an unequal system.[17]

From this perspective, conspiracy theorists like Glenn Beck are partially right in pointing to the hypocrisy and secrecy of the global elites, yet what both sides do not see is that these centrists are not really liberals because they do not base their decisions on reason and impartiality.[18] Although they would like to appear neutral and objective, as Stiglitz shows, they use their knowledge to shield them from considering the facts on the ground. For instance, many interventions into foreign economies fail because they do not consider the underlying social and political factors in the local culture.[19]

Since Stiglitz was often behind many of the policies he is now critiquing, we can read his book as an attempt to heal his centrist guilt.[20] A divided subject, he seeks to get his audience to recognize his moral goodness and his meritocratic competence by revealing what went wrong in formation of globalization:

> IMF structural adjustment policies—the policies designed to help a country adjust to crises as well as to more persistent imbalances—led to hunger riots in many countries; and even when results were not so dire, even they managed to eke out some growth for a while, often the benefits disproportionately to the better-off, with those at the bottom some facing even greater poverty. (xiv)

Similar to the Left's and the Right's criticism of global capitalis admits that the policies that were supposedly produced to hel often ended up mostly aiding the wealthy. One reason for th between intention and effect is that abstract economic theories ideological biases shaped the policies. Still, another factor w; the arrogance of the policy makers and the lack of transparen cies were never corrected.

pain countries had to experience on the way to becoming a successful market economy, and that their measures would, in fact, reduce the pain the countries would have to face in the long run. (xiv)

By making indebted nations open up their markets to foreign interests and requiring them to cut their spending on social welfare programs, the people who were being aided were often harmed as the profits went to the ones in control.[26] Once again, Stiglitz highlights how strong psychological forces prevented more rational and scientific policies from being enacted since the people who were most harmed by these global arrangements were afraid to complain because they had become dependent on financial aid and structured debt reduction. In tun, the global policy elites either ignored the real suffering of the people they were trying to help or they convinced themselves that the pain would be justified in the long run.[27]

THE TRUE GLOBAL ELITE

As Matthew Stewart writes in his *The 9.9%*, upper-middle class professionals often claim to be for a more equal society as they take advantage of inequality.[28] While Stewart focuses on the politics and policies of the United States, we can apply the same psychology to global elites. Even though they may tell themselves that they just want to make the world fairer by reducing suffering and inequality, they often focus on their own careers in an effort at outcompeting others.[29] Meritocracy is, then, undermined by the way that the winners of this system use their gains to make the system work best for their own interests.[30] For instance, highly educated parents spend a great deal of money getting their children into elite universities while they also proclaim their commitment to equity, diversity, and inclusion.[31] Likewise, many of the professors teaching about these issues are elite tenured professors who ignore the fact that most of their colleagues in higher education are instructors with no job security, few benefits, low pay, and no shared governance rights.[32] The centrist meritocratic narcissists believe that since they were successful in the system, the system must be fair.[33]

For Stiglitz, the one thing that does sometimes push people to see that we have a global world with global problems is a major crisis:

> The barbaric attacks of September 11, 2001, have brought home with great force that we all share a single planet. We are a global community, and like

all communities have to follow some rules so that we can live together. These rules must be—and must be seen to be—fair and just, must pay due attention to the poor as well as the powerful, must reflect a basic sense of decency and social justice. In today's world, those rules have to be arrived at through democratic processes; the rules under which the governing bodies and authorities work must ensure that they will heed and respond to the desires and needs of all those affected by policies and decisions made in distant places. (xv)

This vision of global understanding and solidarity should be triggered by our collective knowledge concerning climate change, pandemics, poverty, and war, but the truth is that the global elites often see every catastrophe as an opportunity to impose their particular ideology and policy solutions in a non-transparent way[34]:

> There are no smoking guns here. You won't find hard evidence of a terrible conspiracy by Wall Street and the IMF to take over the world. I don't believe such a conspiracy exists. The truth is subtler. Often it's a tone of voice, or a meeting behind closed doors, or a memo that determines the outcome of discussions. Many of the people I criticize will say I have gotten it wrong; they may even produce evidence that contradicts my views of what happened. I can only offer my interpretation of what I saw. (xv)

Unlike the conspiracy theories on the Right and the Left, Stiglitz does not believe that there is a secret group with a secret plan to control the world; rather, he indicates that elites cannot help but be guided by their internalized ideology and biases, and when these people get together to decide things in a non-transparent way, they undermine democracy and the trust that others will have in the needed institutions.[35]

Responding to Uneven Development

Since most people do not understand how the global economy really functions, they are prone to fill in their missing knowledge with conspiracy theories.[36] One reason for this lack of knowledge is the lack of transparency that Stiglitz describes, but another cause is the way that advances are made in an uneven way:

> Opening up to international trade has helped many countries grow far more quickly than they would otherwise have done. International trade helps eco-

nomic development when a country's exports drive its economic growth. Exported growth was the centerpiece of the industrial policy that enriched much of Asia and left millions of people there far better off. Because of globalization many people in the world now live longer than before and their standard of living is far better. People in the West may regard low-paying jobs at Nike as exploitation, but for many people in the developing world, working in a factory is a far better option than staying down on the farm and growing rice. (4)

A major cause for the populist rejection of globalization has been the fact that economic advancement is often slow and not evenly distributed within and outside of individual nations.[37] The fact of the matter is that while some countries in Asia saw a massive decrease in dire poverty over the last fifty years, other countries in the developed West lost jobs through outsourcing and automation.[38] Moreover, the movement of millions of people to the middle-class in Asia was accompanied by a growing level of wealth inequality globally and in many individual nations.[39] These uneven aspects of development allow the critics to dismiss globalization as a whole instead of clearly seeing what works and what does not work.

A paradox that Stiglitz highlights is that as more people around the world share information through new communication technologies, not only do they gain a stronger sense of being part of a globalized world, but they are also better able to protest against globalization itself:

Globalization has reduced the sense of isolation felt in much of the developing world and has given many people in the developing countries access to knowledge well beyond the reach of even the wealthiest in any country a century ago. The antiglobalization protests themselves are a result of this connectedness. Links between activists in different parts of the world, particularly those links forged through Internet communication, brought about the pressure that resulted in the international landmines treaty— despite the opposition of many powerful governments. (4)

Thus, one of the counter-forces to the control of globalization by the insular global elites is the spread of protests and boycotts around the world.[40] While we do not have a global government with a global opposition party, we do have the ability of oppressed and exploited people to push back through protests and other forms of civil disobedience.[41] Moreover, boycotts are often effective because people can vote with their money as they threaten multinational corporations economically.[42] Yet, as we have seen throughout this book, it is important for the people protesting unfair policies and practices to have a clear understanding of what is actually happening, and this process requires not basing one's perceptions on preconceived theories and ideologies.[43]

Reason and Globalism

It is often said that we should not let the perfect be the enemy of the good, and this notion is very true in relation to global policies and politics.[44] What we need is leaders who are willing to experiment and admit when they are wrong so that complex issues with imperfect information can be addressed. Stiglitz advocates for this type of thinking as he discusses many of the global policies that have helped people make the world more prosperous and just:

> Foreign aid, another aspect of the globalized world, for all its faults still has brought benefits to millions, often in ways that have almost gone unnoticed: guerrillas in the Philippines were provided jobs by a World Bank–financed project as they laid down their arms; irrigation projects have more than doubled the incomes of farmers lucky enough to get water; education projects have brought literacy to the rural areas; in a few countries AIDS projects have helped contain the spread of this deadly disease. (5)

As Stiglitz insists, the problem with our understanding of globalization is that the opponents often dismiss the successes, while the proponents only see success everywhere:

> Those who vilify globalization too often overlook its benefits. But the proponents of globalization have been, if anything, even more unbalanced. To them, globalization (which typically is associated with accepting triumphant capitalism, American style) is progress; developing countries must accept it, if they are to grow and to fight poverty effectively. But to many in the developing world, globalization has not brought the promised economic benefits. (5)

Due to the unbalanced and uneven nature of globalization, I have tried to account for both what has worked and what has not worked. This neutral approach goes against the desire of many to see things as either all good or all bad based on their own ideological perspective.[45]

This need for a democratic, science-based approach to global public policy is the core issue for the future of global politics, but as Stiglitz insists, it is difficult to stop individuals and entire nations from pretending to care about others as they focus on their own needs and gains:

> The critics of globalization accuse Western countries of hypocrisy, and the critics are right. The Western countries have pushed poor countries to eliminate trade barriers, but kept up their own barriers, preventing developing countries from exporting their agricultural products and so depriving them of desperately needed export income. The United States was, of course, one of the prime culprits, and this was an issue about which I felt intensely. When I was chairman of the Council of Economic Advisers, I fought hard against this hypocrisy. It not only hurt the developing countries; it also cost Americans, both as consumers, in the higher prices they paid, and as taxpayers, to finance the huge subsidies, billions of dollars. My struggles were, all too often, unsuccessful. Special commercial and financial interests prevailed—and when I moved over to the World Bank, I saw the consequences to the developing countries all too clearly. (6–7)

In the battle against special interests, Stiglitz documents how hard it is for even someone in the inside to go against a consensus driven by hypocrisy and personal benefit. On one level, it is necessary to expose this hypocritical psychology, but on another level, it is also vital to document the real evidence of global progress. In fact, one reason why I started this book by examining Pinker's documentation of past successes is that in order for us to believe that we can improve things in the future, we have to know what has worked in the past.[46]

How to Make Global Policy Truly Global

One of the most interesting things about the story of global progress is that most people are not aware that it has happened, and so we have to ask how is it possible for advancement to be made when most people remain ignorant about its causes and effects?[47] A possible explanation for this counter-intuitive state of affairs is that much of the progress is generated by social institutions and practices transcending the minds of individual people.[48] For instance, academic research relies on peer review not only because it is important to see if experiments can be replicated but also because a collective process entails more information to be shared.[49] In the logic of crowd-sourcing, a collection of individual minds can often go beyond the ability of isolated thinkers.[50] In terms of global policies, most people do not know or understand how these shared systems work, but these systems still can be very effective. The problem is that if we are ignorant of what causes global progress or even that it has happened, how can we defend the system against those who want to reject it?

It is therefore necessary for us to understand the causes, benefits, and failures of global public policy, and once again, we have to approach this topic in an unbiased way. As Stiglitz reveals, policies often go wrong when they do not fully include the people receiving help in the formation of the solutions:

> Not only in trade liberalization but in every other aspect of globalization even seemingly well-intentioned efforts have often backfired. When projects, whether agriculture or infrastructure, recommended by the West, designed with the advice of Western advisers, and financed by the World Bank or others have failed, unless there is some form of debt forgiveness, the poor people in the developing world still must repay the loans. (8)

It is no wonder that many people in the "Global South" reject globalization: Too often policies designed by elites from the North have failed and placed developing countries in greater debt.[51] Still, the solution is not to give up on global progress; rather, we have to make it more effective by allowing more people to participate in the design and benefits of global policies.

A major issue that Stiglitz brings up is how do you make global policy truly global? Since institutions, like the UN, are often dominated by a handful of developed countries, it is necessary to build a truly global form of government that is democratic and scientific.[52] For Stiglitz, the first part of this process is to more fully understand what globalization actually entails:

> What is this phenomenon of globalization that has been subject, at the same time, to such vilification and such praise? Fundamentally, it is the closer integration of the countries and peoples of the world which has been brought about by the enormous reduction of costs of transportation and communication, and the breaking down of artificial barriers to the flows of goods, services, capital, knowledge, and (to a lesser extent) people across borders. (9)

From this perspective, globalization is much more than international markets: Globalization also relates to the movement of people and ideas around the world.[53] This type of international exchange requires global institutions that can protect individual rights and shared prosperity while extending lifespans and literacy:

> Globalization has been accompanied by the creation of new institutions that have joined with existing ones to work across borders. In the arena of international civil society, new groups, like the Jubilee movement pushing for debt reduction for the poorest countries, have joined long-established organizations like the International Red Cross. Globalization is powerfully driven by international corporations, which move not only capital and goods across borders but also technology. Globalization has also led to renewed attention to long-established international intergovernmental institutions: the United Nations, which attempts to maintain peace; the International Labor Organization (ILO), originally created in 1919, which promotes its agenda around the world under its slogan "decent work" and the World Health Organization (WHO), which has been especially concerned with improving health conditions in the developing world. (9–10)

As Stiglitz illustrates, we have seen the growth of global institutions to deal with global risks and benefits, but these institutions need to be rendered more democratic and effective.[54] What Stiglitz does not call for is a single global government with a single currency and a unified set of policies enforced by one police force and legal system.[55]

The Fear of Global Government

I believe that Stiglitz's resistance to calling for a global government represents a real limitation for his work since many of the problems he exposes can only be solved by the adoption of a single, universal system.[56] For instance, many of the financial crises that he describes are caused by the manipulation of different currencies, and the only real solution to this problem may be the use of a single, global currency.[57] Likewise, since multinational corporations can avoid taxes by declaring the profits in tax-free countries, there is no way to properly tax these wealthy industries.[58] The same goes with labor laws and environmental protections: If individuals and companies can relocate to places with low labor standards and no environmental regulations, then it will be impossible to resolve these problems.[59] Moreover, if we agree that we need universal, global human rights and laws, then we need a global mode of enforcement, and this requires one, integrated government and one shared enforcement system.[60]

As we have seen throughout this book, people on the Left, Right, and center are afraid of a true global government because they believe it concentrates too much power in too few hands as it erases cultural differences and imposes a standardized world from above.[61] However, it is necessary to realize that the only way to fight climate change, pandemics, war, and poverty is to have a global response, and this means that we need to move to a global government. The solution then is to design an international form of governance that is democratic and does not eliminate all cultural differences or individual rights.[62] Perhaps, the first step in this process is to compare a global government to the European Union, which has adopted a single currency and shared set of laws and regulations.[63] Although this system still has its flaws, it has managed to allow for national differences as it enhances shared economic prosperity, health, and safety.[64]

A benefit of the European Union is that it undermines the desire of countries to go to war against each other as they see themselves as part of one collective agency.[65] This move beyond the nation-state as the locus of power shows that it is possible to bring very different cultures under one set of rules without erasing national and ethnic differences. As Stiglitz posits, the roots of the EU stem from the slow development of several international institutions during the twentieth century: "The IMF was founded on the belief that there was a need for collective action at the global level for economic stability, just as the United Nations had been founded on the belief that there was a need for collective action at the global level for political stability. The IMF is a public institution, established with money provided by taxpayers around the world" (12). While the IMF and the UN are far from perfect, they lay the foundation for the formation of a global government based on a single tax system and set of laws and rights.[66]

At one point in his book, Stiglitz does point to the necessity of forming a global government to deal with global problems:

> Today, with the continuing decline in transportation and communication costs, and the reduction of man-made barriers to the flow of goods, services, and capital (though there remain serious barriers to the free flow of labor), we have a process of "globalization" analogous to the earlier processes in which national economies were formed. Unfortunately, we have no world government, accountable to the people of every country, to oversee the

globalization process in a fashion comparable to the way national governments guided the nationalization process. Instead, we have a system that might be called global governance without global government, one in which a few institutions—the World Bank, the IMF, the WTO—and a few players—the finance, commerce, and trade ministries, closely linked to certain financial and commercial interests—dominate the scene, but in which many of those affected by their decisions are left almost voiceless. (21–22)

Since global centrists are often fearful of extreme solutions, they tend to reject this need for a world government, and yet it is hard to see how anything less than a global system of governance will be able to handle the movement of good, labor, and ideas. The issue is then how do make this type of system more transparent, equal, and just?

Stiglitz main solution is to create institutions that will be democratic and rational, and this will require a greater inclusion of developing nations in the decision-making process: "Globalization can be reshaped, and when it is, when it is properly, fairly run, with all countries having a voice in policies affecting them, there is a possibility that it will help create a new global economy in which growth is not only more sustainable and less volatile but the fruits of this growth are more equitably shared" (22). This desire for a more equitable, stable, and sustainable globalization is the only way for us to fight against the global threats of climate change, pandemics, war, and poverty, and so we really do not have a choice. Either we move to a fair and inclusive global government, or we will encounter a mass extinction.[67]

As I will argue in the conclusion to this book, psychoanalysis can help us to develop to psychology we need to defend and promote global progress, but we have to develop a clear understanding of what shapes human morality. Instead of turning to the new brain sciences as the source for our comprehension of human nature, I posit that Freud's work offers the best model for understanding global subjectivity and solidarity.

Notes

1. Stiglitz, Joseph E.. Globalization and Its Discontents (Norton Paperback). W. W. Norton & Company. Kindle Edition.
2. Rickards, James. *The road to ruin: the global elites' secret plan for the next financial crisis*. Penguin, 2016.
3. Samuels, Robert. "Understanding the psychopathology of political ideologies." *Psychoanalysis, Culture & Society* (2023): 1–9.

4. Samuels, Robert, and Robert Samuels. "Beyond Hillary Clinton: Obsessional Narcissism and the Failure of the Liberal Class." *Psychoanalyzing the Left and Right after Donald Trump: Conservatism, Liberalism, and Neoliberal Populisms*(2016): 31–59.
5. Gilboa, Itzhak, Andrew W. Postlewaite, and David Schmeidler. "Probability and uncertainty in economic modeling." *Journal of economic perspectives* 22.3 (2008): 173–188.
6. Stiglitz, Joseph E. "Imperfect information in the product market." *Handbook of industrial organization* 1 (1989): 769–847.
7. Greenwald, Bruce C., and Joseph E. Stiglitz. "Financial market imperfections and business cycles." *The Quarterly Journal of Economics* 108.1 (1993): 77–114.
8. Karnani, Aneel. "Failure of the libertarian approach to reducing poverty." *Asian Business & Management* 9 (2010): 5–21.
9. Stiglitz, Joseph E. "On liberty, the right to know, and public discourse: the role of transparency in public life." *Globalizing Rights: The Oxford Amnesty Lectures 1999* 115 (2003): 135.
10. Stiglitz, Joseph E. *Globalization and its discontents revisited: Antiglobalization in the era of Trump*. WW Norton & Company, 2017.
11. Stewart, Matthew. *The 9.9 percent: The new aristocracy that is entrenching inequality and warping our culture*. Simon and Schuster, 2021.
12. Hedges, Chris. *Death of the liberal class*. Vintage Canada, 2011.
13. Samuels, Robert. "(Liberal) Narcissism." *Routledge Handbook of Psychoanalytic Political Theory*. Routledge, 2019. 151–161.
14. Liu, Catherine. *Virtue hoarders: The case against the professional managerial class*. U of Minnesota Press, 2021.
15. Freud, Sigmund. "A case of obsessional neurosis." *Standard edn* 10 (1909).
16. Ellison, Julie. "A short history of liberal guilt." *Critical Inquiry*22.2 (1996): 344–371.
17. Lawton, John. "The PMC Goes on Trial." *Rhizomes: Cultural Studies in Emerging Knowledge* 37 (2021).
18. Kiersey, Nicholas. "Left anti-politics or left populism? Political distinctions at the end of the end of history." *New Perspectives*30.4 (2022): 389–405.
19. Easterly, William. "Was development assistance a mistake?." *American Economic Review* 97.2 (2007): 328–332.
20. Holmes, Stephen. "Liberal guilt: some theoretical origins of the welfare state." *Responsibility, Rights, and Welfare*. Routledge, 2019. 77–106.
21. Niyonkuru, Fulgence. "Failure of foreign aid in developing countries: A quest for alternatives." *Business and Economics Journal* 7.3 (2016): 1–9.
22. Henrich, Joseph, Steven J. Heine, and Ara Norenzayan. "The weirdest people in the world?." *Behavioral and brain sciences*33.2–3 (2010): 61–83.

23. Chiao, Joan Y., and Bobby K. Cheon. "The weirdest brains in the world." *Behavioral and Brain Sciences* 33.2–3 (2010): 88–90.
24. Marx, Karl. *The German Ideology: A New Abridgement*. Watkins Media Limited, 2022.
25. Erkisi, Kemal, and Turgay Ceyhan. "Trade liberalization and economic growth: A panel data analysis for transition economies in Europe." *Journal of Economics Finance and Accounting* 6.2 (2019): 82–94.
26. Forster, Timon, et al. "How structural adjustment programs affect inequality: A disaggregated analysis of IMF conditionality, 1980–2014." *Social science research* 80 (2019): 83–113.
27. Babb, Sarah. "The social consequences of structural adjustment: recent evidence and current debates." *Annu. Rev. Sociol.* 31 (2005): 199–222.
28. Stewart, Matthew. *The 9.9 percent: The new aristocracy that is entrenching inequality and warping our culture*. Simon and Schuster, 2021.
29. Freeland, Chrystia. "The rise of the new global elite." *The Atlantic* 307.1 (2011): 44–55.
30. McNamee, Stephen J., and Robert K. Miller. *The meritocracy myth*. Rowman & Littlefield, 2009.
31. Liu, Amy. "Unraveling the myth of meritocracy within the context of US higher education." *Higher education* 62 (2011): 383–397.
32. Rysdam, Sheri. "The Political Economy of Contingency." *Teaching English in the Two Year College* 39.3 (2012): A10.
33. McNamee, Stephen J., and Robert K. Miller. *The meritocracy myth*. Rowman & Littlefield, 2009.
34. Klein, Naomi. *The shock doctrine: The rise of disaster capitalism*. Macmillan, 2007.
35. Vašková, Natália, and Vanda Vašková. "Breakdown of trust in financial institutions in light of the global financial crisis." *Journal of Advanced Studies in Finance* 1.1 (2010): 108–114.
36. Willman, C. A. I. "Suspicious constellations: Conspiracy and contingency in postmodern culture (Don DeLillo, Thomas Pynchon, Frederic Jameson)." (1999): 3460–3460.
37. Kyrylych, Khrystyna. "Problem of uneven economic development of the world economy: essence and causes." *Intelektinė ekonomika* 7.3 (2013): 344–354.
38. Saull, Richard. "Rethinking hegemony: Uneven development, historical blocs, and the world economic crisis." *International Studies Quarterly* 56.2 (2012): 323–338.
39. Kniivilä, Matleena. "Industrial development and economic growth: Implications for poverty reduction and income inequality." *Industrial development for the twenty-first century: Sustainable development perspectives* 1.3 (2007): 295–333.

40. Fisher, Dana R., et al. "How do organizations matter? Mobilization and support for participants at five globalization protests." *Social problems* 52.1 (2005): 102–121.
41. Dodson, Kyle. "Globalization and protest expansion." *Social Problems* 62.1 (2015): 15–39.
42. Shi, Wei, and Jingran Wei. "In the crossfire: Multinational companies and consumer boycotts." *China Economic Review* 77 (2023): 101882.
43. Steger, Manfred B. "Ideologies of globalization." *Journal of Political Ideologies* 10.1 (2005): 11–30.
44. Munafò, Marcus. "Don't let the perfect be the enemy of the good." *PLoS Biology* 19.7 (2021): e3001327.
45. Samuels, Robert, and Robert Samuels. "Logos, global justice, and the reality principle." *Zizek and the Rhetorical Unconscious: Global Politics, Philosophy, and Subjectivity* (2020): 65–86.
46. Pinker, Steven. *Enlightenment now: The case for reason, science, humanism, and progress.* Penguin UK, 2018.
47. Samuels, Robert, and Robert Samuels. "The Resistances to Psychoanalysis and Global Progress." *Freud for the Twenty-First Century: The Science of Everyday Life* (2019): 53–67.
48. Barnett, Michael. "International progress, international order, and the liberal international order." *The Chinese Journal of International Politics* 14.1 (2021): 1–22.
49. Roberts, Thomas J., and Jennifer Shambrook. "Academic Excellence: A Commentary and Reflections on the Inherent Value of Peer Review." *Journal of Research Administration* 43.1 (2012): 33–38.
50. Ikediego, Henry Oluchukwu, et al. "Crowd-sourcing (who, why and what)." *International Journal of Crowd Science* 2.1 (2018): 27–41.
51. Dirlik, Arif. "Global South: predicament and promise." *The Global South* 1.1 (2007): 12–23.
52. Fraume, Mabel-Cristina Marulanda, Paula Marulanda Fraume, and Alex H. Barbat. "Evaluating risk from a holistic perspective to improve resilience: The United Nations evaluation at global level." *Safety Science* 127 (2020): 104739.
53. Mir, Usman Riaz, Syeda Mahnaz Hassan, and Mubashir Majeed Qadri. "Understanding globalization and its future: An analysis." *Pakistan Journal of Social Sciences* 34.2 (2014): 607–624.
54. Cornia, Giovanni Andrea. "Globalization and health: results and options." *Bulletin of the World Health Organization* 79 (2001): 834–841.
55. Trachtman, Joel P. *The future of international law: global government.* Cambridge University Press, 2013.
56. Scheuerman, William E. "Review Essay: Global Governance without Global Government? Habermas on Postnational Democracy: The

Postnational Constellation: Political Essays, by Jürgen Habermas. Trans. and ed. by Max Pensky. Cambridge, MA: MIT Press, 2001. 190 pp. 57.50(cloth); 25 (paper). Philosophy in a Time of Terror: Dialogues with Jürgen Habermas and Jacques Derrida, by Giovanna Borradori. Chicago: University of Chicago Press, 2003. 208 pp. 25(cloth); 15 (paper). Time of Transitions, by Jürgen Habermas. Trans. and ed. by Ciaran ...." *Political Theory* 36.1 (2008): 133–151.

57. Rogoff, Kenneth. "Why not a global currency?." *American Economic Review* 91.2 (2001): 243–247.
58. Contractor, Farok J. "Tax avoidance by multinational companies: Methods, policies, and ethics." *Rutgers business review* 1.1 (2016).
59. Arthurs, Harry. "Reinventing labor law for the global economy: The Benjamin Aaron Lecture." *Berkeley J. Emp. & Lab. L.* 22 (2001): 271.
60. Bruggeman, Willy. "International law enforcement co-operation: A critical assessment." *European Journal on Criminal Policy and Research* 9.3 (2001): 283–290.
61. Hoffmann, Stanley. "Thoughts on fear in global society." *Social Research: An International Quarterly* 71.4 (2004): 1023–1036.
62. Bolton, John R. "Should we take global governance seriously." *Chi. J. Int'l. L.* 1 (2000): 205.
63. Laffan, Brigid. "The European Union: a distinctive model of internationalization." *Journal of European Public Policy* 5.2 (1998): 235–253.
64. Telò, Mario, ed. *European Union and new regionalism: regional actors and global governance in a post-hegemonic era.* Ashgate Publishing, Ltd., 2013.
65. Burgess, Michael. *Federalism and European Union: the building of Europe, 1950–2000.* Taylor & Francis, 2000.
66. Güven, Ali Burak. "The IMF, the World Bank, and the global economic crisis: exploring paradigm continuity." *Development and Change* 43.4 (2012): 869–898.
67. Briggs, John C. "Emergence of a sixth mass extinction?." *Biological Journal of the Linnean Society* 122.2 (2017): 243–248.

CHAPTER 6

Conclusion: Psychoanalysis and the Psychology of Global Enlightenment

Abstract This chapter compares Freud's approach to the use of evolutionary psychology in Michael Shermer's book *The Moral Arc*. Although Shermer also believes that global progress has been driven by the use of reason, his turn to a biological model of human nature represents a regressive combination of modern science and premodern fantasy. As is common in the new brain sciences, the formation of a pseudo-science based on biological determinism is coupled with a dismissal of psychoanalysis, and I hope to show how the naturalization of social and psychological structures blocks our ability to fully promote global progress in the future.

Keyword Freud • Michael Shermer • *The Moral Arc* • Human nature • Evolutionary psychology • Brain sciences • Global progress • Naturalization

As a way of concluding this discussion of the relation between psychoanalysis and globalization, I will compare Freud's approach to the use of evolutionary psychology in Michael Shermer's book *The Moral Arc*.[1] Although Shermer also believes that global progress has been driven by the use of reason, his turn to a biological model of human nature represents a regressive combination of modern science and premodern fantasy.[2] As is common in the new brain sciences, the formation of a pseudo-science

© The Author(s), under exclusive license to Springer Nature Switzerland AG 2023
R. Samuels, *Psychoanalysis and the Future of Global Politics*,
https://doi.org/10.1007/978-3-031-41166-3_6

based on biological determinism is coupled with a dismissal of psychoanalysis, and I hope to show how the naturalization of social and psychological structures blocks our ability to fully promote global progress in the future.[3]

Past Illusions

In *The Future of an Illusion*, Freud defines illusions as false representations generated from an internal desire: "Such ideas, which put themselves forward as dogmas, are not deposits from experience or end products of cogitation, they are illusions, fulfilling the oldest, most powerful, most pressing desires of the human race; the secret of their strength is the strength of those desires" (29).[4] The key move here is to argue that cultural and personal illusions are based on imaginary wish fulfilments; moreover, these illusions are not the products of experience or thought. Instead, they are derived from our oldest and most powerful desires.

One of the things that Freud finds so destructive regarding religious illusions is that they produce a false imaginary global moral order of universal justice:

> Through the gracious action of divine providence fear of the perils of life is allayed, the appointment of a moral world order guarantees fulfilment of the demand for justice that has so often remained unfulfilled within human culture, while prolonging earthly existence by means of a future life provides the spatial and temporal framework within which such wish-fulfilment shall occur. (30)

As an Enlightenment thinker, Freud knows that morality and justice are the result of human thought, actions, and institutions and not the product of some divine power or natural order.[5] In other words, if we want to pursue universal human rights, we can only rely on our own social constructions.[6]

It is interesting that when Freud tries to define the exact meaning of an illusion, he turns to the growing rise of German nationalism in the 1920's as his prime example: "It is possible to describe as an illusion the assertion made by certain nationalists that the Indo-Germanic race is the only one capable of culture ..." (30). By tying nationalism to the formation of an illusion, Freud locates the same type of mental processes in religion and nationalistic ideologies.[7] In both cases, an imaginary conception of the world is driven by a primal desire.

Freud believes it is important to distinguish psychotic delusions from religious and nationalistic illusions because unlike psychotic productions, illusions are defined by the fact that they cannot be proven or disproven: "The reality value of most of them cannot be assessed. Just as they are unverifiable, they are also irrefutable" (31). While modern science is defined by the ability of verifying or disproving its findings, illusions are impossible to prove or disprove.[8] In fact, some have argued that psychoanalysis itself cannot be a science because its theories cannot be verified, but this is clearly untrue.[9] We can show through experimental methods that people lie to themselves and that they believe in things based on their desires. We can also show that the neutrality of the analyst helps people to speak more freely without self-censorship and that some people cannot control their own impulses or accept the reality of their lives.[10]

The fact of the matter is that psychoanalysis is a true science, while, as she shall see, many of the new brain sciences are pseudo-sciences because they are based on the mistaken idea that all our thoughts and social institutions are all the result of evolutionary selection.[11] For instance, many evolutionary psychologists believe that humans today are controlled by mental programs inherited through natural selection and derived from our distant hunter-gatherer ancestors.[12] One problem with this theory is that it requires knowing exactly what problems people faced hundreds of thousands of years ago and what solutions allowed them to survive and reproduce. Not only do we have to read the minds of people today, but we have to be able to read the minds of people from the distant past in order to determine what automatic mental programs shape their thoughts and actions.[13] It is also hard to prove or disprove these theories because we need to go back in time in order to see what people were actually thinking and doing.[14]

Evolutionary psychology and many versions of neuroscience refuse to distinguish between the mind and the brain as a way of eliminating culture and individual psychology from their analysis.[15] Since they believe that we are preprogrammed by natural selection to think and act in certain ways, they do not have to bother with culture, education, or individual differences.[16] Even when they try to include environmental factors, they usually end up relying on a theory that anything that is fast and intuitive must be inherited, and any inherited program must be universal and therefore void of cultural influence.[17] Since it takes a very long time for natural selection to weed out unsuccessful behavior, evolutionary psychology has to reject the importance of contemporary ideology or recently invented human interventions.[18]

Non-Evolved Evolutionary Theory

In *The Moral Arc*, Shermer attempts to use evolutionary psychology to account for global progress, and one way that he makes this argument is by claiming that the goal of global progress is survival, and only evolution can explain what allows us to survive: "Any organism subject to natural selection—which includes all organisms on this planet and most likely on any other planet as well—will by necessity have this drive to survive and flourish ..." (11). The subtle shift here involves what is meant by survival.[19] From a biological perspective, survival entails the rate of reproducing specific genetic material.[20] Although the carrier of this material has to survive to a certain age in order to reproduce, evolution is about the long-term, species-level replication of inherited traits.[21] What people tend to confuse is the difference between the survival of particular individuals and the survival of specific genetic structures. For example, in the theory of the selfish gene, the idea is not that our genes make us selfish; rather, the only function of genes is to replicate themselves.[22] Genetic material, then, has no purpose or design beyond self-replication, and so it is misguided to compare individual humans to genes since we have intentions, and as psychoanalysis has shown, we often do not focus on doing what helps us survive and reproduce on the species level.[23]

In fact, much of Freud's work reveals how we subvert our biological nature.[24] Not only do we engage in sexual activity not directed towards reproduction, but we imagine things that do not exist and structure our institutions through the use of shared beliefs and necessary but impossible ideals.[25] Yet, evolutionary psychologists are so bent on basing human nature and social institutions on biology that they eliminate the fundamental differences between minds and brains on the one hand and humans and other animals on the other hand.[26] One place where this lack of distinctions is apparent in the notion that morality is not based on thoughts, language, or education: "Our moral consideration should be based not primarily on what sentient beings are thinking, but on what they are feeling" (12). By getting rid of thought from the moral realm, Shermer is able to make the absurd claim that all other animals and beings also have morality: "The neural pathways of emotions, for example, are not confined to higher-level cortical structures in the brain, but are found in evolutionarily older subcortical regions. Artificially stimulating the same regions in human and nonhuman animals produces the same emotional reactions in both" (12). Since Shermer wants to base morality on emotions and not thought, he is able to repress the difference between humans and other animals, and one of the problems with this lost distinction is that it undervalues the need for humans to create artificial social institutions based on reason and well-thought-out social policy.[27]

In *Psychoanalyzing the Politics of the New Brain Sciences*, I have argued that evolutionary psychology and neuroscience often unintentionally end up supporting a Right-wing ideology because of the way they naturalize social hierarchies and focus on isolated individuals competing for scarce resources.[28] In Shermer's case, we see how his emphasis on the survival of individuals makes him disregard group identities and collective issues: "It is the individual who is the primary moral agent—not the group, tribe, race, gender, state, nation, empire, society, or any other collective—because it is the individual who survives and flourishes, or who suffers and dies. It is individual sentient beings who perceive, emote, respond, love, feel, and suffer—not populations, races, genders, groups, or nations" (12). This view of morality can be seen as Right-wing because it mimics the backlash against the Leftist interest in race, gender, and class.[29] In fact, many of the proponents of the brain sciences dismiss the social sciences for not being scientific and for replacing empirical analysis with political ideology. The fact of the matter is that new disciplines like evolutionary psychology hide their underlying politics behind a veil of supposed scientific neutrality.

I do not think that Shermer would consider himself to be a supporter of Right-wing ideology, but his use of biological determinism pushes him to privilege the isolated individual over any type of group identity: "Historically, immoral abuses have been most rampant, and body counts have run the highest, when the individual is sacrificed for the good of the group" (12). This criticism of group behavior dovetails with the Right-wing focus on individual identity and the rejection of identity politics based on minority groups.[30] Shermer goes as far as claiming that the advancement of human rights has not been driven by minority-based social movements but instead has been centered on the rights and freedoms of individuals:

> The Rights Revolutions of the past three centuries have focused almost entirely on the freedom and autonomy of individuals, not collectives—on the rights of persons, not groups. Individuals vote, not races or genders. Individuals want to be treated equally, not races. Rights protect individuals, not groups; in fact, most rights (such as those enumerated in the Bill of

Rights of the US Constitution) protect individuals from being discriminated against as members of a group, such as by race, creed, color, gender, and—soon—sexual orientation and gender preference. (13)

Shermer's claim here is clearly far removed from unbiased, neutral science as he makes the strange argument that the collective civil rights, gay rights, and women rights movements were about protecting autonomous individuals. I think he misreads history because he needs to emphasize the biological determinism of individuals, and he desires to promote a false form of liberal democracy.[31] Rather than seeing that universal human rights often protects individuals by prohibiting discrimination against their particular group, he insists that only individuals are protected.[32] We find this same tendency to dismiss the importance of minority-based social movements in Pinker's work, which may reflect on the way that a commitment to evolutionary psychology devalues collective politics based on group identity.[33]

Just as the libertarian Right is centered on the freedom and pleasure of the autonomous individual coupled with the criticism and rejection of group identity politics, Shermer's evolutionary psychology pushes him to misunderstand the foundation of modern globalizing human rights:

> This drive to survive is part of our essence, and therefore the freedom to pursue the fulfillment of that essence is a natural right, by which I mean it is universal and inalienable and thus not contingent only upon the laws and customs of a particular culture or government. Natural rights theory arose during the Enlightenment to counter the belief in the divine right of kings, and became the basis of the social contract that gave rise to democracy, a superior system for the protection of human rights. (13)

Although it is true that modern democratic constitutions often promote natural rights, it is clear that these rights have to be produced and maintained by social groups.[34] Furthermore, while universal human rights represent a globalization of modern liberal democratic values, this form of universalization is a human ideal and not a product of some shared biological force.[35] Shermer misunderstands this constructed aspect of universality so that he can promote both individual liberty and biological determinism: "In rights language, the individual is imbued with personal autonomy. As a natural right, the personal autonomy of the individual gives us criteria by which we can judge actions as right or wrong: do they increase or decrease the survival and flourishing of individual sentient beings?" (14). In coupling survival with individual autonomy, Shermer seeks to have it both ways since we have to ask, how can someone be free if they are determined by their genes?[36]

This contradiction between determinism and individual autonomy runs throughout Right-wing libertarian ideology.[37] After all, how can markets represent individual freedom if they are reliant on the negotiation between supply and demand? Due to the fact that capitalism is based on exchange value, it is never a question of the total autonomy of the isolated individual.[38] Although Right-wing libertarian ideology likes to promote a fantasy of total freedom and unregulated enjoyment, the truth is that free markets are still a social mechanism used to mediate between people.[39] In fact, Marx argued that Darwin based his theory of evolution on the industrial British economy, which combined a bottom-up competition for scarce resources with a sorting and survival mechanism.[40]

A key aspect of evolutionary psychology is the notion that every thought and social institution, like free markets, are the result of natural selection:

> We are all born with a moral sense, with moral emotions that guide us in our interactions with other people, and that are influenced by local culture, customs, and upbringing. Nature endowed us with the capacity to feel guilt for the violation of promises and social obligations, for example, but nurture can tweak the guilt dial up or down. Thus morality is real, discoverable, "out there" in nature, and "in here" as part of our human nature. From these facts we can build a science of morality—a means of determining the best conditions to expand the moral sphere and increase moral progress through the tools of reason and science. (14)

In this passage, Shermer does at least admit that culture and education can influence natural tendencies, but the emphasis is still on the way society and psychology are based on biology.[41]

What is so fascinating about Shermer's work is that he combines a commitment to modern science and reason with an investment in a fake science that fails to live up to the standards of the scientific method:

> Understanding the nature of things and the causes of effects is what science is designed to do, and ever since the Scientific Revolution there has been a systematic effort by thinkers in all fields to apply the methods of science—which include the philosophical tools of reason and critical thinking—to understanding ourselves and the world in which we live, including and espe-

cially the social, political, and economic worlds, with an end toward the betterment of humanity. This effort has produced a worldview known as Enlightenment Humanism (or secular humanism, or simply humanism), which, unlike most other worldviews, is more a method than an ideology; it is a means of solving problems more than it is a set of doctrinaire beliefs. (14)

It would be hard to disagree with Shermer's claim here that global progress is based on the scientific method applied to human issues, but why does he feel it necessary to return to biology and a distorted version of evolutionary theory to support his analysis?[42] Of course, the use of science lends credibility to his arguments, but the danger is that by employing a pseudo-science he misrecognizes what will allow us to sustain and extend global progress in the future. If we do not recognize that it is humans working tougher to produce social institutions, which often go individual desires and feelings, then we will be unable to defend the social practices making globalization work more effectively.

Although at times, Shermer does argue that reason is the foundation of global progress, at other times, he insists that social morality is based on emotional intuitions derived from natural selection: "Reason is the cognitive capacity to establish and verify facts through the application of logic and rationality, and to make judgments and form beliefs based on those facts. Rationality is the application of reason to form beliefs based on facts and evidence, instead of guesswork, opinions, and feelings. That is to say, the rational thinker wants to know" (16). This clear definition of reason as the guiding force behind modern science and democracy is undermined by his insistence that it is not cognition or logic that guides morality but feelings inherited by biology.[43]

This conflict between reason and emotion is brought out in the open in the following passage:

> However, as several decades of research in cognitive psychology has shown, we are not the rationally calculating beings we'd like to think we are, but are instead very much driven by our passions, blinded by our biases, and (for better or worse) moved by our moral emotions. The confirmation bias, the hindsight bias, the self-justification bias, the sunk-cost bias, the status-quo bias, anchoring effects, and the fundamental attribution error are just a few of the many ways that our brains work to convince us that what we want to be true is true—regardless of the evidence—in a general process called "motivated reasoning." Nevertheless, the capacity for reason and rationality

is within us as a feature of our brains that evolved to form patterns and make connections (it's called learning) in the service of survival and flourishing in the environment of our evolutionary ancestry. (16)

At the start of this passage, Shermer posits that we are not as rational as we think we are since we are often guided by bias and moral emotions. Here, it does appear that he is privileging reason over emotion as he sees our moral feelings as just getting in the way. However, much of his book is centered on proving that we need to be guided by our moral emotions derived from natural selection.[44]

Since evolutionary psychologists and neuroscientists usually focus on examining the brains of individuals, they have a hard time recognizing the social practices and institutions transcending the isolated individual.[45] In terms of global progress, what is often missing from the accounts given by the new brain sciences is the way that needed policies and collective organizations go beyond the desires and feelings of the brains located in separate individuals. In other words, social systems add something extra to the combination of individual brains, and this added element is an artificial component not determined by biology or evolution.[46] Yet, Shermer wants to insist that even our most artificial social practices are driven by natural selection:

> Pinker calls this an open-ended combinatorial reasoning system that "even if it evolved for mundane problems like preparing food and securing alliances, you can't keep it from entertaining propositions that are consequences of other propositions." This ability matters for morality because "if the members of species have the power to reason with one another, and enough opportunities to exercise that power, sooner or later they will stumble upon the mutual benefits of nonviolence and other forms of reciprocal consideration, and apply them more and more broadly. (16)

The complicated idea here is that even if natural selection was first only dedicated to helping individuals survive, the mental functions that survived are able to be used for unintended purposes.[47] Once again, the problem with this theory is that it does not account for the fact that people are born into a world with certain social structures and laws that they cannot control or ignore. Moreover, to be a subject of society, one must suspend one's own self-interest, and this process has nothing to do with natural selection.

Since Shermer cannot accept the psychoanalytic idea that human thought and culture allows us to make a radical break with biology and evolution, he constantly returns to the idea that we are guided by isolated brains determined by natural forces:

> Louis Liebenberg has, in fact, argued that our ability to reason scientifically is a by-product of fundamental skills for tracking game animals that our ancestors developed. Liebenberg's analogy between tracking and the scientific method is revealing: "As new factual information is gathered in the process of tracking, hypotheses may have to be revised or substituted by better ones. A hypothetical reconstruction of the animal's behaviors may enable trackers to anticipate and predict the animal's movements. These predictions provide ongoing testing of hypotheses. (16–17)

According to this perspective, non-human animals must also have science because they know how to track other animals through a process of trial and error. Yet, animals do not think, and they do not have complicated communication and social systems.[48] By trying to equate the scientific method with animal behavior, Shermer undermines our ability to understand the foundations of modern science and human reason.

When Shermer does document the causes of global progress, he returns to artificial human constructs: "Flynn and his colleague William Dickens suggest that the increases in cognitive reasoning may have started centuries ago with the Industrial Revolution, which saw an improvement in both the quantity and quality of education, better nutrition, disease control, and the manipulation of complex machinery" (24). Since education is often pitted against inherited natural programs, it should be clear that the advancements in science, health, and technology are not the result of natural evolution; rather, people working together solve problems through thought, testing, and communication.

Since Shermer wants to base his argument on evolutionary psychology *and* the documentation of human history, he ends up constantly contradicting himself as he moves between biological and social determinism: "Thinking like a scientist means employing all our faculties to overcome our emotional, subjective, and instinctual brains to better understand the true nature of not only the physical and biological worlds, but the social world (politics and economics) and the moral world (abstracting how other people should be treated) as well" (25). I would tend to support this argument because it explains how we have to fight against our moral biases derived from evolution, but most of his book bases social morality on biology.

Returning to Freud

Since Shermer believes that psychoanalysis is a pseudo-science, he does not recognize all of the ways Freud's theory offers a more accurate understanding of human reason, emotion, and global progress.[49] Towards the end of *The Future of an Illusion*, Freud ponders if his criticism of religion will affect how people see psychoanalysis, and he responds that it does not matter since the goal of analysis is to present an impartial view on any subject matter: "In reality, psychoanalysis is a method of research, an impartial tool—like, say, infinitesimal calculus. If a physicist should use the latter to work out that, after a certain time, the earth will perish, people will nevertheless hesitate to ascribe destructive tendencies to the calculus itself and outlaw it accordingly" (37). From Freud's perspective, science should pursue the truth no matter where it leads—even if people will attempt to block it or even outlaw it.

By opposing science to religion, the founder of psychoanalysis argues that religion cannot be the path to a more just, fair, and happier world:

> It is doubtful whether, at the time when religious teachings held unrestricted sway, the human race was happier, by and large, than it is today; it was certainly no more moral. People have always known how to trivialize the rules of religion, thereby thwarting their intention. Priests, whose role it was to monitor obedience to religion, helped them in this. God's goodness inevitably spiked the guns of his righteousness, as it were: people sinned, then they made sacrifice or did penance, then they were free to sin again. (38)

From Freud's perspective, religion fails to break the cycle between transgression and guilt, and so it is necessary to develop a social morality that is not based on some higher power or natural order.[50]

Instead of arguing for a direct conflict between religion and science, modernity has relied on the gradual displacement of illusions with facts. Thus, as the world becomes more scientific, it also becomes more secular, and this process enables the spread of global progress.[51] For Freud, there is no way to stop the globalization of scientific understanding because in the long-run the truth of reality always prevails:

> The scientific mind generates a specific way of approaching the things of this world; faced with the things of religion, it pauses, hesitates, and finally here too steps over the threshold. The process is unstoppable, the more people have access to the treasures of our knowledge, the more widespread the severance from religious belief—at first only from the outdated, offensive fashions in which it is kitted out, but then also from its fundamental premises. (39)

Freud's commitment to science and reason should not be under-estimated, and so it is ironic that psychoanalysis has been represented as being unscientific, while evolutionary psychology has gained the reputation of being a real science.

Form Freud's perspective, the globalization of scientific reason often goes on undetected, and this partially due to the way that science does not take on ideological beliefs and illusions in a direct manner: "Culture has little to fear from educated persons and those who work with their intellect. The replacement of religious motives for cultural behaviour by other, secular ones would in their case proceed in silence; moreover, they are themselves for the most part upholders of culture" (39). Through this silent spread of science, reason, and secular humanism, Freud sees a new mode of morality being developed, which no longer relies on the illusions of a higher power or a predetermined natural order; instead, Freud affirms that humans develop social morality and social institutions through human interaction and communication: "So it would be an undoubted advantage to leave God out of it altogether and frankly concede the purely human origin of all cultural institutions and rules" (42). As a necessary aspect of universal human rights, it is important to understand the human origin of social practices and institutions without turning to biology or religion.[52]

Freud adds that when we stop ascribing morality to religious belief, we will be able to make rules that are more just, fair, and understandable:

> Along with the holiness to which they lay claim, the rigidity and immutability of such commandments and laws would also fall away. People would be able to understand that such precepts had been created not so much to keep them under control, rather to serve their interests; they would gain a more cordial attitude towards them, seeking less to overturn them, more to improve them. (42).

Instead of seeming morality as imposed by religion or natural selection, Freud affirms that it is more beneficial for people to comprehend how humans have made these laws and norms through free social interaction.

Freud's view of global progress is greatly influenced by this theory that the development of societies matches the development of individuals, and so the same things that allow children to overcome their original illusions and immorality will also help societies advance:

> one might assume that, during its centuries-long evolution, the human race as a whole gets into states that are like neuroses—and for the same reasons, namely because in the eras when it languished in ignorance and was intellectually weak it produced the drive-renunciations essential to human coexistence through purely affective forces alone. The fall-out from quasi-repressive processes occurring in primeval times clung to culture for a long time to come. Religion, in this reading, is the universal human obsessional neurosis; like the child's, it stemmed from the Oedipus complex, the relationship to the father. Accordingly, a turning away from religion must be expected to occur with the fateful inexorability of a growth process, and we (in this view) are in the throes of that phase of evolution right now. (43–44)

Since Freud draws a parallel between individual and social development, it is necessary to ask how can best promote global progress?[53] It is clear that we cannot put the world on the couch and let everyone free associate into they discover the truth of their lives; rather, we have to continue to defend reason and the modern institutions based on rationality.

Notes

1. Shermer, Michael. *The Moral Arc*. Henry Holt and Co.. Kindle Edition.
2. Hagen, Edward H. "Evolutionary psychology and its critics." *The handbook of evolutionary psychology* 1 (2015).
3. Samuels, Robert. *Psychoanalyzing the politics of the new brain sciences*. Springer, 2017.
4. Sigmund Freud. *The Future of an Illusion*. Penguin Books Ltd. Kindle Edition.
5. Samuels, Robert, and Robert Samuels. "Logos, global justice, and the reality principle." *Zizek and the Rhetorical Unconscious: Global Politics, Philosophy, and Subjectivity* (2020): 65–86.
6. Gregg, Benjamin. *Human rights as social construction*. Cambridge University Press, 2011.

7. Freud, Sigmund. *Mass psychology*. Penguin UK, 2004.
8. Swinburne, R. G. "Falsifiability of scientific theories." *Mind* 73.291 (1964): 434–436.
9. Schwartz, Joseph. "What is science? What is psychoanalysis? What is to be done?." *British Journal of Psychotherapy* 13.1 (1996): 53–63.
10. Ellis, Albert. "An introduction to the principles of scientific psychoanalysis." *Genetic Psychology Monographs* (1950).
11. Brinkmann, Svend. "Can we save Darwin from evolutionary psychology?." *Nordic Psychology* (2011).
12. Buller, David J. *Adapting minds: Evolutionary psychology and the persistent quest for human nature*. MIT press, 2006.
13. Holcomb, Harmon R. "Just so stories and inference to the best explanation in evolutionary psychology." *Minds and Machines* 6 (1996): 525–540.
14. Hubálek, Michal. "A brief (hi) story of just-so stories in evolutionary science." *Philosophy of the Social Sciences* 51.5 (2021): 447–468.
15. Samuels, Robert. "Neuroscience and the Repression of Psychoanalysis." *(Mis) Understanding Freud with Lacan, Zizek, and Neuroscience*. Cham: Springer International Publishing, 2022. 29–62.
16. Hagen, Edward H. "Invariant world, invariant mind. Evolutionary psychology and its critics." *Handbook of evolutionary psychology, Volume 1: Foundations* (2014): 136–160.
17. Samuels, Robert, and Robert Samuels. "The Brain Sciences Against the Welfare State." *Psychoanalyzing the Politics of the New Brain Sciences* (2017): 85–114.
18. Rose, Steven, Richard Charles Lewontin, and Leon Kamin. "Not in our genes: Biology, ideology and human nature." *The Wilson Quarterly* 152 (1984).
19. Rose, Steven, Richard Charles Lewontin, and Leon Kamin. "Not in our genes: Biology, ideology and human nature." *The Wilson Quarterly* 152 (1984).
20. Dawkins, Richard. *The selfish gene*. Oxford university press, 2016.
21. Gardner, Andy, and John J. Welch. "A formal theory of the selfish gene." *Journal of Evolutionary Biology* 24.8 (2011): 1801–1813.
22. Werren, John H., Uzi Nur, and Chung-I. Wu. "Selfish genetic elements." *Trends in Ecology & Evolution* 3.11 (1988): 297–302.
23. Poeldinger, W. J. "The psychopathology and psychodynamics of self-destruction." *Crisis: The Journal of Crisis Intervention and Suicide Prevention* (1989).
24. Shepherdson, Charles. *Vital signs: Nature, culture, psychoanalysis*. Psychology Press, 2000.
25. Harari, Yuval Noah. "Sapiens: a brief history of humankind by Yuval Noah Harari." *The Guardian* (2014).

26. Panksepp, Jaak, and Jules B. Panksepp. "The seven sins of evolutionary psychology." *Evolution and cognition* 6.2 (2000): 108–131.
27. Gannon, Linda. "A critique of evolutionary psychology." *Psychology, Evolution & Gender* 4.2 (2002): 173–218.
28. Samuels, Robert. *Psychoanalyzing the politics of the new brain sciences.* Springer, 2017.
29. Samuels, Robert, and Robert Samuels. "The Backlash Politics of Evolutionary Psychology: Steven Pinker's Blank Slate." *Psychoanalyzing the politics of the new brain sciences* (2017): 35–58.
30. Epstein, Richard A. "The dangerous allure of libertarian paternalism." *Review of Behavioral Economics* 5.3–4 (2018): 389–416.
31. Wilkinson, Will. "A Declaration of Cognitive Independence?." (2006).
32. Flowers, Nancy. *Human Rights Here and Now: Celebrating the Universal Declaration of Human Rights.* Human Rights USA Resource Center, 229 19th Avenue South, Suite 439, Minneapolis, MN 55455, 1998.
33. Carroll, Joseph. "Evolutionary social theory: The current state of knowledge." *Style* 49.4 (2015): 512–541.
34. Flew, Antony. "Could There Be Universal Natural Rights?." *The Journal of Libertarian Studies* 6.3–4 (1982): 277–288.
35. Samuels, Robert, and Robert Samuels. "Logos, global justice, and the reality principle." *Zizek and the Rhetorical Unconscious: Global Politics, Philosophy, and Subjectivity*(2020): 65–86.
36. Peters, Ted. *Playing God?: Genetic determinism and human freedom.* Routledge, 2014.
37. Berofsky, Bernard. *Determinism.* Princeton University Press, 2015.
38. Amariglio, Jack, and Antonio Callari. "Marxian value theory and the problem of the subject: The role of commodity fetishism." *Rethinking Marxism* 2.3 (1989): 31–60.
39. Frank, Thomas. *One market under God: Extreme capitalism, market populism, and the end of economic democracy.* Anchor, 2001.
40. Ball, Terence. "Marx and Darwin: A reconsideration." *Political Theory* 7.4 (1979): 469–483.
41. Pinker, Steven. *The blank slate: The modern denial of human nature.* Penguin, 2003.
42. Lobato, Emilio JC, and Corinne Zimmerman. "The psychology of (pseudo) science: Cognitive, social, and cultural factors." *Pseudoscience: The conspiracy against science* (2018): 21–43.
43. Miller, Christian B. "On Shermer on morality." *Annals of the New York Academy of Sciences* 1384.1 (2016): 63–68.
44. Turner, Jonathan H. "Natural selection and the evolution of morality in human societies." *Handbook of the Sociology of Morality* (2010): 125–145.

45. Legrenzi, Paolo, and Carlo Umiltà. *Neuromania: On the limits of brain science*. Oxford University Press, 2011.
46. Misulia, Mark. "Aping Mankind: Neuromania, Darwinitis, and the Misrepresentation of Humanity." *First Things: A Monthly Journal of Religion and Public Life* 223 (2012): 65–67.
47. Gould, Stephen Jay. "Exaptation: A crucial tool for an evolutionary psychology." *Journal of social issues* 47.3 (1991): 43–65.
48. Latimer, Joanna, and Mara Miele. "Naturecultures? Science, affect and the non-human." *Theory, Culture & Society* 30.7–8 (2013): 5–31.
49. Samuels, Robert, and Robert Samuels. "Logos, global justice, and the reality principle." *Zizek and the Rhetorical Unconscious: Global Politics, Philosophy, and Subjectivity* (2020): 65–86.
50. Rieff, Philip. *Freud: The mind of the moralist*. University of Chicago Press, 1979.
51. Cady, Linell E., and Elizabeth Shakman Hurd. "Comparative secularisms and the politics of modernity: An introduction." *Comparative secularisms in a global age* (2010): 3–24.
52. Donnelly, Jack. *Universal human rights in theory and practice*. Cornell University Press, 2013.
53. Freud, Sigmund. *Totem and taboo*. Phoemixx Classics Ebooks, 2021.

INDEX

A
Abandonment, 52, 53
Addiction, 10, 53, 61, 62
Aggression, 35, 60
Ambivalence, 10
Analyst, 8, 17, 20, 35, 42, 44–46, 95
Animals, 7, 25, 96, 97, 102
Anthropomorphism, 23
Anti-social, 19, 40, 59
Anxiety, 10
Asia, 81

B
Backlash, 4, 7, 11, 97
Beck, Glenn, 3, 54–65, 77
Bias, 7, 8, 10, 28, 34, 41, 42, 77, 80, 100, 101, 103
Biden, Joe, 54, 59
Binary oppositions, 10, 52
Biology, 36, 96, 99–104
Borderline personality disorder, 52, 54
Bosch, Carl, 6
Brain sciences, 4, 87, 93, 95, 97, 101

C
Capitalism, 3, 7, 8, 10, 15, 28, 34–36, 38, 39, 42–45, 53, 55, 57, 60–63, 65, 75, 77, 82, 99
Centrist liberals, 34, 53, 55, 73, 74
China, 4, 64, 65
Church, 25
Civilization, 16, 18–20
Class, 11, 21, 22, 34, 35, 38, 40–42, 45, 52, 53, 55, 58, 63, 76, 78, 79, 97
Climate change, 2–4, 11, 16, 22, 23, 25, 28, 55, 58, 60, 63, 64, 80, 86, 87
Colonialism, 39
Conservative ideology, 2, 15, 19, 27
Conspiracy theories, 2, 3, 52, 53, 55–62, 64, 65, 76, 80
Consumer capitalism, 10
Corporations, 10, 52, 53, 55–60, 63, 65, 81, 85
Counter-revolution, 59
COVID-19, 6, 58
Culture wars, 55

© The Author(s), under exclusive license to Springer Nature Switzerland AG 2023
R. Samuels, *Psychoanalysis and the Future of Global Politics*,
https://doi.org/10.1007/978-3-031-41166-3

D

Darwin, Charles, 37, 38, 99
Davos, 55, 58
Death drive, 2
Debt, 79, 84, 85
Defense mechanisms, 2, 8, 9, 15, 51, 52, 54, 57
Democracy, 3, 4, 7, 10, 15, 20, 26, 28, 34–36, 39–44, 60, 62, 64, 76, 80, 98, 100
Democratic law, 3, 7, 10, 28, 40, 41, 65
Denial, 2, 10, 25, 52, 53
Descartes, Renee, 28, 45
Desire, 10, 16, 18, 20, 24, 25, 28, 34, 41, 44, 52, 54, 59, 61, 62, 65, 77, 78, 80, 82, 86, 87, 94, 95, 98, 100, 101
Developing nations, 78, 87
Dialectical, 10, 26, 34, 40
Disavowal, 52
Diversity, 36, 39, 77, 79
Dogma, 27, 28, 94

E

Ego ideal, 20, 21, 37
Emotion, 96, 99–101, 103
Empathy, 10
Equality, 5, 7, 8, 19, 34, 40–42, 45, 46, 59, 74
Equity, 77, 79
Ethnic, 5, 26, 27, 34, 86
Europe, 64
European Union (EU), 64, 86
Evil, 9, 10, 35, 36, 43, 56
Evolution, 37, 38, 96, 99, 101–103, 105
Evolutionary psychology, 4, 93, 95–99, 102, 104
Exploitation, 19, 37, 38, 43, 44, 81
Extremism, 58

F

Fact-based public policy, 34
Fantasy, 2, 52, 53, 56, 59, 63, 75, 93, 99
Fascism, 60, 62–65
Feudalism, 6, 7
Foreign aid, 82
Fox News, 59
Free association, 8, 27, 34, 42
Freedom, 19, 26, 36, 40, 42, 43, 52, 54, 56, 59, 97–99
Freud, Sigmund, 2, 3, 8–10, 15–28, 34, 36–40, 52, 56, 59, 61, 75, 77, 87, 93–96, 103–105
Fundamental fantasy, 9, 52, 53, 56

G

Gender, 8, 35, 40–42, 45, 97, 98
Genetics, 37, 96
Global economy, 57, 58, 73, 74, 80, 87
Global elite, 3, 52, 55, 60, 62, 63, 65, 73–87
Global government, 11, 22, 81, 85–87
Global politics, 33, 39, 83
Global progress, 1–11, 17, 23–26, 28, 35, 42, 64, 74, 83, 84, 87, 93, 94, 96, 100–103, 105
Global South, 84
Global Studies, 35
Government regulations, 6, 63
Great Reset, The, 55, 57–65
Guilt, 36, 60, 77, 99, 103

H

Haber, Fritz, 6
Hegel, Georg, 45
Henrich, Joseph, 78
Higher education, 78, 79

INDEX

Human nature, 20, 36, 37, 87, 93, 96, 99
Hyperbole, 35, 54, 57, 64
Hypnosis, 25, 61
Hypocrisy, 55, 58, 60, 75, 77, 78, 83
Hysteria, 9, 11, 35

I
Id, 37, 53
Ideal ego, 21
Idealization, 23, 40
Ideals, 3, 7, 8, 17, 19–22, 34, 37, 41, 42, 44–46, 75, 96, 98
Identification, 9, 10, 22, 35, 36, 42, 54–58, 60, 62
Identity, 9, 10, 21, 22, 27, 35, 36, 41, 42, 45, 52, 97, 98
Ideology, 2, 11, 15, 17–19, 26, 27, 34, 35, 44, 52–55, 58, 62, 64, 65, 74–76, 80, 82, 94, 95, 97, 99, 100
Illusions, 94–95, 103–105
IMF, 75–78, 80, 86, 87
Impersonal, 7, 24, 42, 43
Incomplete information, 75
Individualism, 7, 19, 33, 35, 40, 43, 44, 59
Inequality, 3, 8, 38, 41, 65, 74, 77, 79, 81
Innocent, 9, 35, 36, 54, 56
Instinctual renunciation, 22, 23, 25
Introspection, 3, 8, 17, 19, 56

J
Journalism, 58
Justice, 24, 26, 34, 42, 80, 94

K
Kant, Immanuel, 16, 26
Kernberg, Otto, 54
Knowledge, 16, 17, 19, 23, 77, 78, 80, 81, 84, 104

L
Labor laws, 85
Lacan, Jacques, 21, 45
Left-wing, 3, 10, 11, 35, 38, 40–42, 44, 45, 52, 59
Liberal, 4, 10, 11, 33–35, 40–44, 52, 53, 55, 58–60, 62, 64, 73, 74, 76, 77, 98
Liberalism, 3, 40
Libertarian, 3, 59, 63, 75, 98, 99
Local culture, 77, 99
Love, 25, 97

M
Marginalized, 21, 34, 35, 41
Marxism, 18
Masochism, 11
Mass media, 56
Medicine, 6, 34, 35, 37, 39, 41
Meritocracy, 79
Middle class, 63, 81
Mirror stage, 21
Modern, 3, 4, 7, 8, 10, 11, 16, 17, 19, 26, 27, 34–36, 38–43, 45, 46, 64, 65, 74, 76, 93, 95, 98–100, 102, 105
Monarchy, 6, 7
Morality, 26, 87, 94, 96, 97, 99–101, 103–105
Moral order, 94
Multinational corporations, 56, 57, 60, 63, 65, 81, 85

N

Narcissism, 11, 20–22, 76–79
Nationalism, 2, 15, 21, 22, 26, 27, 64, 94
Nation-state, 86
Naturalization, 94
Natural selection, 95, 96, 99–101, 105
Nature, 3, 7, 16–18, 20, 22–25, 36, 37, 42, 43, 45, 82, 87, 93, 96, 99, 102
Neurosis, 39, 42, 77, 105
Neutrality, 2–4, 8, 11, 17, 27, 28, 34, 38, 40–46, 95, 97
Newton, Isaac, 36
Non-judgment, 42

O

Objectivity, 42, 51
Obsessive-compulsive, 77
Oedipus Complex, 10, 52, 59, 105
Other, the, 35

P

Pandemics, 3, 4, 6, 22, 23, 25, 28, 58, 60, 63, 80, 86, 87
Paranoia, 53, 56, 60
Patriarchy, 35
Philosophy, 4, 33, 34, 36, 38, 43
Phobia, 2
Pinker, Steven, 2, 4–6, 8, 83, 98, 101
Pleasure principle, 10, 52
Poetry, 24
Political rally, 25
Postmodern, 7, 8, 10
Poverty, 3, 4, 8, 25, 27, 28, 36, 40, 43, 53, 60, 63, 65, 76–78, 80–82, 86, 87
Premodern, 2, 3, 6, 7, 10, 26, 40, 65, 93
Primal horde, 52

Primary processes, 2, 53, 54, 56, 57
Projection, 52–54, 56, 63
Projective identification, 54–58, 60, 62
Propaganda, 62
Pseudo-science, 93, 95, 100, 103
Psychopathology, 3, 17, 52–54, 57, 74, 76–79

R

Race, 23, 25, 35, 38, 40–42, 45, 94, 97, 98, 103, 105
Racism, 5, 38, 40, 43, 60
Rationality, 20, 75, 100, 105
Reagan, Ronald, 58
Reality principle, 2, 8, 16, 17, 28, 56
Real, the, 2, 5, 8, 10, 11, 22–24, 53, 58, 60–63, 65, 76, 78, 79, 83, 85
Reason, 3, 6–9, 17, 20, 22, 24, 26–28, 37, 38, 42, 52, 57, 58, 63, 75–77, 80, 82–83, 93, 97, 99–105
Recognition, 21
Religion, 6, 7, 9, 16, 24–27, 39, 41, 94, 103–105
Repression, 2, 9, 35, 39
Resentment, 57, 58
Resistance, 2, 7, 17, 22, 26, 34, 53, 85
Right-wing, 3, 10, 11, 51–61, 63, 64, 97, 99

S

Sacrifice, 20–23, 26, 27, 103
Schwab, Klaus, 57
Science, 2–4, 6, 7, 10, 11, 15–17, 20, 25–28, 34–39, 41, 42, 44, 45, 65, 74, 76, 83, 87, 93, 95, 97–104
Self-interest, 28, 39, 42, 101
Sexism, 43
Shame, 36, 60, 77

Shermer, Michael, 3, 93, 96–103
Social construction, 94
Social hierarchies, 2, 7, 10, 19, 38–40, 97
Socialist, 54, 59, 63
Social movements, 6, 8, 10, 41, 97
Social regulation, 18, 59
Solidarity, 22–24, 64, 80, 87
Splitting, 10, 35, 52–56
Stewart, Matthew, 79
Stiglitz, Joseph, 3, 73
Structural adjustment, 77, 78
Subject, 21, 25, 26, 34, 36, 42, 45–46, 59, 62, 77, 84, 96, 101, 103
Subjectivity, 3, 4, 26, 39, 42, 87
Suggestion, 56, 61, 62
Super-ego, 37, 53
Survival, 37–39, 96, 97, 99, 101

T

Taxes, 53, 54, 59, 63, 85, 86
Tax revolt, 59
Therapy, 44
Totalitarian, 54, 55, 59, 62–65
Tradition, 7, 10, 26, 33, 34, 39, 43
Transference, 26
Trump, Donald, 59
Truth, 2, 7, 16, 17, 19, 28, 52, 61, 65, 78, 80, 99, 103, 105

U

Unconscious, 2, 11, 21, 24, 52–54, 57
Understanding, 2–4, 8, 11, 16, 17, 22, 36, 39, 44, 53, 80, 82, 87, 99, 103
United Nations (UN), 4, 64, 84–86

United States, 11, 27, 56, 60, 62, 64, 79, 83
Universal human rights, 2–4, 10, 17, 27, 34, 41, 46, 94, 98, 104
Universality, 26, 28, 40–43, 45, 98
Unreason, 17, 20
Upper-middle class, 11, 52, 76, 79

V

Victim fantasy, 2, 56
Victim identification, 52, 56
Victim identity, 9
Violence, 24, 35, 62
Virtue signaling, 11, 77

W

Walls, Gary, 3, 33–40, 42–44
War, 4, 6, 9, 22, 25, 28, 55, 60, 63, 80, 86, 87
Wealth, 5, 28, 52, 59, 81
Wealthy, 10, 43, 45, 52, 53, 55, 57–60, 65, 77, 85
Welfare programs, 5, 63, 79
West, the, 53, 65, 81, 84
Western, Educated, Industrial, Rich, Democratic (WEIRD), 78
Working class, 52, 53, 55, 58, 62
World Bank, 73, 83, 84, 87
World Economic Forum (WEF), 55, 57, 58, 65
WTO, 87

Z

Zizek, Slavoj, 45–46, 61